EXTRAORDINARY FOODS

for the
Everyday Kitchen

by the authors of
FEAST WITHOUT YEAST and
AN EXTRAORDINARY POWER TO HEAL

LORI KORNBLUM and
BRUCE SEMON, M.D., Ph.D.

**More than 125 Original, New Recipes
and More than 60 Menus to Astound &
Amaze You**

Delicious, Simple & Easy

- sugar-free
- yeast-free
- wheat-free
- milk-free
- soy-free
- all Kosher

Wisconsin Institute of Nutrition, LLP
Milwaukee, Wisconsin
www.nutritioninstitute.com

DISCLAIMER

Extraordinary Foods for the Everyday Kitchen describes relationships that have been observed between the common yeast, *Candida Albicans*, certain foods, and medical conditions, and provides recipes that are yeast free, gluten free and casein free. It is not intended as medical advice specific to any particular person. Its intention is solely informational and educational for the public and the medical profession. Treatment of health disorders, including those which appear to be yeast connected, must be supervised by a licensed health care professional. Either you or the health care professional who examines and treats you, must take responsibility for uses made of this book. This book is not intended to create legal advice for any particular person, nor is it intended to create an attorney-client privilege. The authors and the publisher cannot take medical or legal responsibility of having the contents of this book considered as a prescription for everyone. The authors and publisher have neither liability nor responsibility to any person or entity with respect to any loss, damage, or injury caused or alleged to be caused by the information contained in this book.

EXTRAORDINARY FOODS FOR THE EVERYDAY KITCHEN
Wisconsin Institute of Nutrition, LLP
http://www.nutritioninstitute.com

copyright (c) 2003 by Bruce Semon, M.D., Ph.D. and Lori Kornblum

Cover design and graphic consultation: Tiffany Navins, Graphic Ingenuity
Cover art: Jeanine Semon, http://www.jeaninesdream.com
Book design: Lori Kornblum and Sarah Semon

Library of Congress Catalog in Publication Data:

Semon, Bruce, M.D., Ph.D., and Lori Kornblum
  Extraordinary Foods for the Everyday Kitchen
  Includes index
    1. Candida Related Complex 2. Candida Diet
    3. Gluten Free Diet 4. Casein Free Diet
    5. Allergy Diet 6. Soy Free Recipes
    7. Milk Free Recipes 8. Wheat Free Recipes
    9. Autistic Disorder 10. Allergies

Library of Congress Control Number: 2003106369
ISBN 0-9670057-7-9
First Edition   September, 2003   10 9 8 7 6 5 4 3 2 1

To order single copies or to schedule author appearances, contact us at 1-877-332-7899, or http://www.nutritioninstitute.com. email: bsemon@nutritioninstitute.com.

About the Authors

Dr. Semon and Ms. Kornblum are the authors
of *Feast Without Yeast:4 Stages to Better Health*
(1999), and *An Extraordinary Power to Heal* (2003),
to which this book is a companion. *Feast Without
Yeast* has sold thousands of copies and is available
throughout the world.

Dr. Bruce Semon is board certified psychiatrist
and child psychiatrist, as well as a doctorate level
nutritionist, practicing in Milwaukee, Wisconsin. He
received his M.D. from University of Wisconsin-Madi-
son and his Ph.D. in Nutrition from University of Cali-
fornia-Davis. Dr. Semon was a Research Fellow in the
Laboratory of Nutritional and Molecular Regulation, of
the National Cancer Institute at the National Institutes
of Health. He received his adult and child psychiatry
training at the Medical College of Wisconsin.

Dr. Semon has published several academic papers
relating to nutrition, and is a contributing author to
Biological Treatments for Autism and PDD, by Dr.
William Shaw.

As a complement to Dr. Semon's regular psychiatry
practice, Dr. Semon has treated many patients for
yeast-related illnesses, including all of the medical
conditions described in this book, with remarkable
results. Dr. Semon speaks regularly to support groups

and conferences about the connection between what people eat and their health. Dr. Semon accepts new patients.

Lori Kornblum is an attorney practicing in Milwaukee, Wisconsin. She has published scholarly and popular articles relating to law. Ms. Kornblum has taught cooking classes to implement special diets and speaks about how to change diet.

Dr. Semon and Ms. Kornblum are married and live in Milwaukee with their three children, one of whom has an autistic disorder.

Dr. Semon and Ms. Kornblum both are available for speaking engagements and consultations. For more information about becoming a patient of Dr. Semon, or for information about speaking engagements or consultations, please call toll free 1-877-332-7899, or write to us at support@nutritioninstitute.com.

Acknowledgments

We gratefully acknowledge the assistance of E'liane Khang for her assistance in editing this book, as well as Tiffany Navins, Graphic Ingenuity, for her creative input, and cover design. We thank artist Jeanine Semon for her inspirational cover artwork.

We especially acknowledge our children, friends and relatives who have been "testing" these recipes day in and day out. Their comments have shaped the book and guaranteed that all of the recipes are ones that real people, in their everyday kitchens, can easily cook and proudly serve the recipes in this book. Our children especially have helped develop menus and recipes. Our daughter Sarah Semon also contributed her tremendous creative ability to helping design this book.

Although we created most of the recipes in this book in our kitchen, we were fortunate in having others contribute recipes to this book. They are acknowledged on the recipes they contributed. These friends and relatives are E'liane Khang, Jeanine Semon, Vannie Lee Henning and Joan Gertel.

Finally, we acknowledge the readers and fans of our first book, Feast Without Yeast:4 Stages to Better Health (Wisconsin Institute of Nutrition, LLP, 1999), who took the time to tell us what they wanted in a second book! Because of their comments, Extraordinary Foods for the Everyday Kitchen has a chapter containing more than 60 menus that you can use for all occasions.

This book is dedicated to our children,

Avi
Sarah
and Mikah

who have tasted, tested and enjoyed all of these recipes
and offered their advice on most of them!

Contents

Introduction

Extraordinary Foods for the Everyday Kitchen is no ordinary cookbook. It is an adventure in eating. In this book, you will find tantalizing recipes made from wonderful, easily available ingredients. You also will find nutritional information and interesting notes and observations. This chapter is your guide through the book. We tell you:

☆ Why we Wrote *Extraordinary Foods for the Everyday Kitchen*

☆ How to use the Nutritional Information in each Recipe

☆ Information about particular ingredients (a "Note on Ingredients")

☆ Cooking tips

☆ Further Resources from Wisconsin institute of Nutrition, LLP

Why did we write *Extraordinary Foods for the Everyday Kitchen*?

We wrote it for you--the person who is searching for outstanding, easy recipes to make every day. You don't have to be on a special diet to enjoy this book. We have many readers of our first book, *Feast Without Yeast: 4 Stages to Better Health* (Wisconsin Institute of Nutrition, LLP, 1999) who do not follow any special diet, but incorporate our recipes into their everyday cooking.

We also wrote *Extraordinary Foods for the Everyday Kitchen* for our family. We have been following the 4 Stages diet for more than eight years. We introduced the 4 Stages diet in *Feast Without Yeast*, and explained it further in *An Extraordinary Power to Heal* (Wisconsin Institute of Nutrition, LLP, 2003). *Extraordinary Foods for the Everyday Kitchen* is the companion cookbook to *An Extraordinary Power to Heal. Extraordinary Foods* can help you implement the changes in your diet that you want to make.

So we have experienced ourselves the 4 Stages diet and years of "fine tuning" the delicious recipes that follow its guidelines.

Nearly all of the recipes in this cookbook were created in our kitchen, for our family and friends. A few of the recipes were created by others. We are thankful to those people, and acknowledge those contributions in the individual recipes.

Finally, we wrote this book for Dr. Semon's patients, and for the thousands of people who use our 4 Stages diet to improve their health.

You will find that this truly is an "everyday" cookbook. We use no exotic ingredients that you will need to mail order or search for high and low. You can find all of the ingredients to make our recipes in regular food stores or local health food stores. You will find more than 125 exciting original and delicious recipes, as well as more than 60 menus for all occasions, in response to our many readers who requested help in planning meals around our many delicious recipes.

We hope that you will enjoy using this book as much as we enjoyed creating the recipes and menus!

Nutritional Information

All of the recipes in *Extraordinary Foods for the Everyday Kitchen* are completely:
- ☆ **Yeast, Mold and Fermentation Free**
- ☆ **Wheat/Gluten Free**
- ☆ **Milk/Casein Free**
- ☆ **Soy Free, Rye Free and Corn Free**
- ☆ **Sugar Free**
- ☆ **Kosher**
- ☆ **Preservative Free**
- ☆ **Dye Free**

Each recipe has nutritional information contained in a gray box just beneath the title. The gray box looks something like this:

> Yeast Free • Wheat/Gluten Free
> Milk/Casein Free • Egg Free • Cholesterol Free
> STAGE IV

The box contains nutritional information related to diets free of yeast, wheat or gluten, milk or casein, eggs and cholesterol.

"Yeast Free" means that the recipe is entirely free of yeast, mold and fermented foods. **All of the recipes in *Extraordinary Foods* are free of yeast, mold and fermented foods.**

"Wheat/Gluten Free" means that the recipe is entirely free of all wheat products, and also is free of grains containing gluten, a protein found in wheat, barley, oats and some other grains. **All of the recipes in *Extraordinary Foods* are free of wheat and gluten.**

"Milk/Casein Free" means that the recipe is free of milk and the milk protein casein. **All of the recipes in *Extraordinary Foods* are free of milk and casein.** Occasionally we use butter in recipes. The box will say "Milk/Casein Free (without butter)." This means that if you use safflower oil instead of butter, the recipe is free of milk and casein. Using butter on a casein free diet is controversial because butter may contain trace amounts of casein, a milk protein. We use small amounts of butter with no ill effects. However, if you do not want to use butter, we have in every recipe a non-butter alternative.

If you believe you are sensitive to casein and butter is harmful to your health, please consult your health care professional before using butter.

"Egg Free" means that the recipe is completely free of eggs.

"Cholesterol Free" means that the recipe is completely free of cholesterol.

"Suitable through Stage IV" tells you something about the 4 Stages diet, described in *Feast Without Yeast* and *An Extraordinary Power to Heal*. The 4 Stages diet is a system for eliminating the foods that most harm your health, and substituting foods that are better for you. The diet eliminates foods slowly and gradually. People following the diet start with Stage I, the most harmful foods. Many people never need to go beyond Stage I. Those who need to continue to Stage II will eliminate more harmful foods. Stage III eliminates wheat and milk containing foods. Stage IV eliminates some additional foods. The 4 Stages diet transitions people very gradually from their "normal" diet to one that is healthier for their bodies. The gradual transition is critical to being able to stick to this change in eating. Each stage builds on the previous stages. Stage I is the least restrictive, Stage II eliminates more foods and incorporates Stage I; Stage III eliminates wheat/gluten and milk/casein, but incorporates Stages I and II. Stage IV eliminates a few more foods, and incorporates Stages I through III. Because we thoroughly describe the diet and explain how to use it in other books, we do not do so here. If you are following the 4 Stages diet, you can cook every recipe in this cookbook, regardless of which stage you are on. **All of the recipes in *Extraordinary Foods* are suitable through Stage IV.**

In addition to the nutritional information in the gray boxes, you should know that **all of the recipes in *Extraordinary Foods* are free of refined sugar, artificial dyes and preservatives, and common allergens including corn, rye and soy.**

All of the recipes are **completely kosher**, and are either meat recipes or parve (neither meat nor dairy.) All of the recipes without meat are or can be made parve.

A Note on Ingredients

Beans

All recipes use dried beans unless otherwise noted.

Whenever possible, buy dried beans instead of canned beans, remembering the simple rule: if you don't prepare the food, you won't know what's in it. Moldy beans are quite common. Canned beans potentially contain beans that were moldy when canned, which spreads the mold to the entire can. You can visually inspect dried beans to eliminate the especially bad ones.

Beans are best purchased in bulk from cooperatives or health food stores or grocery stores with high product turnover. You can purchase beans in packages from supermarkets that have high turnover. You can order beans in 25 pound bags to save money and shopping time.

We recommend two basic cooking methods for beans: the slow-cooker method and the "quick soak" method. We do not recommend the conventional "overnight soak" method, because it increases the risk of fermentation. We like to cook beans in the slow cooker because that method requires the least preparation, the least watching, and no boil-overs. Slow cooking also seems to decrease gas from beans.

Slow Cooker Method for Cooking Beans

Use this method for kidney, black, small red, large red, and garbanzo beans. Do not use this for navy beans, lentils, or other soft beans.

Place the beans in the slow cooker. Cover the beans with about three to four times as much water as beans. Cover. Cook on higher heat until the beans are soft, usually several hours or overnight. Reduce to medium heat and continue cooking until you need the beans. The beans taste best after about 24 hours, but are good for snacks after 12 hours. Drain the beans in a colander and rinse before serving or using in other recipes.

Quick soak method for Cooking Beans

This method is faster than the slow cooker and is more suitable for soft beans, such as navy beans and canellini beans (white kidney beans).

Place two to three cups of beans in a large pot. Cover with sufficient water, using the chart on the next page. Bring to a boil. Remove from heat. Allow the beans to soak in the hot water for one hour. Cast off the water. Replace with fresh water. Bring the beans to a boil and cook for the amount of time shown in the chart below.

Beans (1 c. dry)	Amt. Water (in cups)	Cooking Time	Yield (cups)
Anasasi	3	2.5 hours	2
Black Turtle	3	1.5 hours	2
Garbanzo (chick peas)	4	4 hours	3
Kidney	3	2 hours	2
Lentils	2.5	45 minutes	2
Navy	3	1.5 hours	2

Using the Precooked Beans

Now that you have some cooked beans, what do you do with them? There are many recipes for beans throughout *Extraordinary Foods for the Everyday Kitchen*, and many more in *Feast Without Yeast*. One of our favorite ways to serve beans is to stir-fry them or serve them mixed with a little sea salt and safflower oil as a snack. The stir-fry combinations are almost infinite. Just have beans available and use your imagination!

Cooking Spray

Occasionally, you may want to use nonstick cooking spray to grease pans. Be sure you use cooking spray that is acceptable for your Stage of the 4 Stages diet. We recommend canola oil cooking spray or safflower oil cooking spray. Olive oil cooking spray is acceptable as well. Look carefully at the ingredients.

Fruit--Fresh and Freshly Frozen

Some recipes use fresh or freshly frozen fruit. Good rules of thumb are: avoid packaged fruit (except berries and cranberries), use only fruit in season, and make sure the fruit is firm and ripe, but not soft and overripe. After purchasing the fruit, check carefully for mold or rot and cut out the bad spots.

We purchase fresh berries in season (raspberries, blueberries, blackberries and cranberries) and freeze them. To freeze, spread the berries on cookie sheets or in pans so the berries are one layer thick and not touching each other. Stack the pans in the freezer for 12-24 hours until the berries are frozen solid. Store in zipper type freezer bags. Date the bags and use within the year.

Herbs and Spices

All recipes use dried herbs, unless the recipe specifically states "fresh" herbs. If you wish to use fresh herbs instead of dried herbs, use three times the amount of fresh herbs as dried. For example, instead of using 1 teaspoonful of dried dill, use 3 teaspoonsful of fresh dill.

All green herbs are acceptable. These include herbs such as dill, basil, marjoram, thyme, oregano, chervil, and so on. Dill seeds, sesame seeds and celery seeds also are fine.

Avoid the colored spices, including cinnamon, cumin, curry powder, mustard powder, garlic powder, cardomon, allspice, cloves, mace, and so on. These spices can be OK on occasion, especially through Stage I. You should determine, based on your own experience, whether you can tolerate these spices. Please follow our general advice: **if you know you are sensitive to these spices, PLEASE DO NOT USE THEM.**

Honey

We recommend only fresh, unprocessed honey. This is "natural" honey. Processed honey has been heated and has fewer nutrients available than unprocessed honey. Processed honey looks very clear compared with unprocessed honey. Supermarket brands, such as Sue Bee, are processed.

Natural honey comes in more than 200 flavors, depending on which types of flowers the bees found. Our personal preference is clover honey, a light and sweet honey. However, we encourage you to experiment with different flavors to see which ones you like best. Some honeys are very strong (buckwheat, for example). Others are more tart, like cranberry honey. The taste of the recipe will change according to the flavor of the honey you use.

Natural honey usually is available at farmers' markets, food cooperatives, health food stores and some supermarkets. If you can get to a farmer's market where the honey farmer sells his or her own products, you will get the best honey at the best price and the best information about the honey. Don't be afraid to ask questions! You want to know whether the honey has been heated and when the honey was bottled. Try to get this year's honey. You can purchase honey in bulk and transfer it to smaller jars, saving shopping time and money.

Lemon Juice

Our recipes use freshly squeezed lemon juice. Keep a stock of fresh lemons on hand, or, when you find lemons at a good price, squeeze the juice by hand or machine and freeze it for later use. We recommend freezing the juice in ice cube trays. Put the cubes in a zipper-type of freezer bag and use within a year.

NEVER USE BOTTLED LEMON JUICE, even if the juice is in a cute container and says "freshly squeezed." You do not know if the bottlers used an old fermented lemon in the mix, or how "fresh" is "fresh."

Oil

Our recipes use only expeller pressed safflower oil. You may use olive oil or canola oil on occasion.

"Expeller pressed" describes the method of extracting the oil from the plant. All vegetable oils are derived naturally through a process called "expeller pressing" or through a synthetic process using a petrochemical solvent. Expeller pressing involved putting seeds through a washing or steaming process, then pressing them, at low temperatures, to squeeze out the oils. The oil is then filtered to remove seed meal, and bottled. These oils are labelled "expeller pressed" or "mechanically pressed" or "unrefined." Under current labelling laws, the manufacturer need not state the method of extraction.

We recommend only expeller pressed oil because the oil is better for you. First, synthetic extraction processes often use high heat and/or chemicals, which may cause cancer causing compounds to be formed. Second, adding chemicals is not necessarily beneficial to health.

Safflower oil also is recommended because it is better for you than other oils. The safflower plant, and thus the oil, is less likely to be mold contaminated than corn or olive oil. Safflower oil also contains all of the essential fatty acids.

Safflower oil comes in several grades. It ranges from very light to very dark in appearance. The darker the oil, the more robust the flavor. We prefer the lighter grade of safflower oil, because the flavor does not overpower the other flavors in a recipe. Experiment and determine for yourself which flavors you like best.

Other people studying and writing about yeast free diets may differ from the recommendation to use safflower oil as the primary oil. They do not believe that safflower oil is bad, but prefer olive and canola oil.

Olive and canola oils may be used on the 4 Stages diet. Experiment with the recipes for taste. All of these oils have distinct flavors, so you may need to adjust the recipes for flavor. Soy oil may be used if you are 100% positive that whomever is eating your food is not sensitive to soy.

Some oils are unacceptable. They are cottonseed, corn and peanut oil. Cottonseed oil is mold contaminated, and contains other poisons that have been shown to cause heart disease in animals. Corn and peanuts are often mold contaminated.

Other researches have written about using other types of fats and oils, and their nutritional benefits. Some of the information they put forth may contradict some of the information in this book, but these are good references.

For a general reference, see Dr. William Crook's book, *The Yeast Connection Handbook.* Dr. Crook summarizes the results of such noted researchers as Dr. Sidney Baker, Dr. Leo Galland and Dr. Laura Stevens. Dr. Baker's book, *Detoxification and Healing,* and Dr. Udo Erasmus' book, *Fats that Heal and Fats that Kill*, also discuss fats and oils. Finally, Dr. James Balch and Phyllis A Balch have written a comprehensive guide to nutritional healing, called *Prescription for Nutritional Healing.* This is an excellent general reference book.

Potatoes

Most recipes specify the types of potatoes to use, because different types of potatoes have different flavors and textures. The most common potatoes are red potatoes and russet potatoes.

Red potatoes, sometimes called "new potatoes," are firm and have a sweet, creamy flavor and texture when cooked.

Russet potatoes have brown skins. They have a fluffier, grainer texture when cooked.

There are many other types of potatoes, including Superior Whites, purple potatoes, Yukon Golds, and others. Experiment with different potatoes to see which ones you like best.

Purchase only the best quality potatoes. Peel the potatoes to eliminate mold on the skin. Cut the potatoes to check for bad spots inside. Cut out any bad spots.

Do not use potatoes that are soft or green, or which have actively growing sprouts.

Rice Pasta

Most pasta is made from wheat. However, on a gluten/wheat free diet, wheat is not acceptable. We have found that rice pasta substitutes nicely for wheat pasta. You will find that people love the flavor of rice pasta.

A note of caution based on much experience: cook the rice pasta exactly according to the package directions. Otherwise, you will under or overcook it.

Several companies make rice pasta. Our personal preference is Pastariso. This brand is approved for use by people with Celiac disease and/or an intolerance to gluten products. Pastariso makes rice pasta in many different shapes and sizes. It generally is available in health food stores and food cooperatives, and in some supermarkets. For more information, contact:

Rice Innovations, Inc.
1773 Bayly Street
Pickering, ontario
Canada L1W2Y7

Pumpkin

Pumpkin-based recipes in this book turn out best when you use fresh pumpkin. Use canned pumpkin only when you are not able to use fresh pumpkin. The best cooking fresh pumpkins are pie pumpkins, available in the fall. They are small and sweet. If pie pumpkins are not available, use whatever pumpkins you can find.

One small pumpkin (10 inches diameter) usually makes enough pureed pumpkin for about two and a half cups of puree, about two small pies. If you like to plan ahead, get your pumpkins in the fall. Freeze or can pureed pumpkin for use later in the year.

Fresh pumpkin can be prepared in the microwave oven, regular oven or on the stove. Microwaving takes less time and is easier, but you lose the seeds, which are delicious roasted and salted. Please see the recipe on page 172.

Rice

Our recipes use only whole grain rice, such as brown rice or red rice. Usually we use long grain brown rice. This is the most common brown rice. We use whole grain rice because it is more nutritious, and more delicious, than white rice. All rice grows with a thin outer covering. This covering contains some of the fiber, and all of the vitamins and minerals in the rice. Processors make white rice by removing this nutrient-rich covering from the brown rice. Brown rice has more nutrients, more fiber, and much more flavor than white rice. If you never have used brown rice, you are in for a treat!

Because brown rice tastes different than white rice, we recommend starting by substituting brown rice for white rice slowly. Start with 1/4 cup of brown rice for every 3/4 cups of white rice (for one cup total). Then increase to half and half, then to 3/4 brown and 1/4 white. After a few weeks, you will become accustomed to the different flavor and texture of brown rice.

Red rice is a type of wild rice. We have seen "Wehani" red rice and "Himalayan" red rice. Red rice opens up like barley and becomes fluffy when cooked. It adds texture and a nutty flavor to foods.

Sea Salt

This book uses only "sea salt" for salt. We do not use regular table salt. Sea salt tastes different from regular table salt because it is totally natural. Sea salt contains all of the minerals that you need, including iodine. Commercial table salt contains additives such as dextrose, a sugar, and it lacks minerals except in some cases added iodine. If you cannot find sea salt, substitute table salt. However, be aware that the recipe will taste different. Add the salt a little at a time, tasting between additions, to make sure that you add only what you need.

Our recipes tend to be well salted. If you do not care for salt, or are on a severely restricted low so-dium diet, use your common sense and start with less salt, adding salt to taste as you go.

Here are some basic tips for making cooking easier, more delicious and more efficient:

☆ Read the recipe before you start cooking.

☆ Chop large vegetables, such as carrots, zucchini, celery, and so on, as you go. In recipes that call for many types of chopped vegetables that are sauteed or stir-fried in a particular order, chop the first vegetables, start them cooking, then chop the next vegetable while the first is cooking, add it when needed, and continue from there.

☆ Chop small items, such as garlic, ginger and scallions, in advance.

☆ Do not mince unless the recipe calls for mincing. Chop the vegetables large, especially in recipes you will puree in the end.

☆ Heat the pot or pan prior to adding food. The food will cook faster and taste better.

☆ Use the amount of oil the recipe requires. Do not skip or skimp on the oil, especially in soups. Oil adds a huge amount of flavor for a small number of calories distributed through an entire recipe.

Additional Resources from Wisconsin Institute of Nutrition, LLP

To learn more about the 4 Stages diet, see our books *Feast Without Yeast: 4 Stages to Better Health* (Wisconsin Institute of Nutrition, LLP: 1999), and *An Extraordinary Power to Heal* (Wisconsin Institute of Nutrition, LLP: 2003).

Both books are available from Wisconsin Institute of Nutrition, which you can call toll free at 1-877-332-7899. They also are available from Amazon.com and many book stores and health food stores.

In addition to giving you dietary information, *An Extraordinary Power to Heal* shows you how foods affect your health. This book gives case studies of many different medical conditions that patients were told were hopeless, but which they were able to heal using anti-yeast therapy and dietary changes. These conditions include fibromyalgia, Chronic Fatigue Syndrome, autism, ADD and ADHD, headaches, food addition, allergies, ear infections, eczema and psoriasis and more.

Feast Without Yeast has more than 225 original recipes, as well as specific advice for parents about how to handle special diets for children, including handling picky eater, lists of recipes kids love, and other information.

Please feel free to contact us at support@nutritioninstitute.com, and check our website, http://www.nutritioninstitute.com.

Soups

Soups are great any time, anywhere. We often start with soup, or even have soup as the main meal. In warm weather or cold, soup is always welcome at our table. In this chapter, you will find a wide variety of soups, all of which are vegetarian except the soups in the section "Soups with Meat." You will find tantalizing recipes, from our dairy-free creamy soups to our rich and hearty cholents, from our chunky vegetable soups to our soups flavored with meat.

☆   Creamy Soups

☆   Chunky Vegetable Soups

☆   Cholents

☆   Soups with Meat

Carrot Ginger Soup

Yeast Free • Wheat/Gluten Free
Milk/Casein Free • Egg Free • Cholesterol Free
STAGE IV

This is an all time hit. It is sweet and spicy, especially on cold winter days. Or just anytime. "This is really wonderful! A perfect fall soup that is so good!" This recipe is made for a 3 quart pot. If using a 6 quart pot, double the recipe exactly, except water. Use 14 c. water.

2 T. expeller pressed safflower oil

1/2 c. chopped scallions

1 T. chopped fresh ginger root

2-1/2 c. sliced or chopped peeled carrots

3 c. peeled and cubed (1/2 inch) red potatoes

10 c. water

1-1/2 tsp. sea salt

Heat the oil in a 3 quart pot. When the oil is hot, **add** the scallions. **Saute** until scallions are soft. Then add the ginger; saute for about 30 seconds. **Add** the carrots; saute until carrots are soft. **Add** the potatoes; **saute** a few minutes. Add water and salt. Cover, bring to a **boil**, then reduce to a **simmer**. When potatoes and carrots are cooked, about 20 to 30 minutes, puree and serve! This soup can be doubled exactly for a larger group. Use a 6 quart pot to cook.

Cream of Celery Soup

Yeast Free • Wheat/Gluten Free
Milk/Casein Free • Egg Free • Cholesterol Free
STAGE IV

Non-dairy cream soups are a real treat. This is a very strong celery soup, for celery lovers only!

 2 T. expeller pressed safflower oil

 1 large leek, chopped

 1 bunch celery, chopped, including leaves (about 6-7 c.)

 1 T. sea salt

 1/8 tsp. black pepper

 1 tsp. celery seed

 9-10 medium red or Yukon Gold potatoes, peeled and cubed

 water

Heat the oil in a 6 quart pot. When the oil is hot, **add** the leek and celery. **Saute** until celery is soft. **Add** the salt, pepper, celery seed and potatoes. Add water to within 1 inch of the top of the pot. Cover. Bring to a **boil**. Reduce to a **simmer**. Cook until the potatoes are soft. **Puree** the soup. This soup purees better in a regular blender than with a hand blender. **Taste** for salt and add more if desired.

Carrot, Leek and Broccoli Soup

Yeast Free • Wheat/Gluten Free
Milk/Casein Free • Egg Free • Cholesterol Free
STAGE IV

This is an unusual soup, a hearty vegetable soup. Don't skip the steps of sauteing the vegetables! This cooking technique imparts flavor to the soup.

> 2 T. expeller pressed safflower oil
>
> 2 large leeks, sliced in rounds
>
> 2-1/2 lb. carrots, peeled and chopped into 2 inch chunks
>
> 1/2 lb. broccoli, cut into florets (about 3 c.)
>
> 1 T. sea salt
>
> 1 T. dried basil
>
> 12 c. water
>
> 3 T. freshly squeezed lemon juice

Heat the oil in a 6-quart kettle. When the oil is hot, add the leeks. **Saute** until soft. **Add** the carrots. **Saute** until bright. Add the broccoli, basil and salt. Saute until the broccoli is soft. Add the water. Cover. Bring to a **boil**, reduce to **simmer**. **Cook** at least one hour. This soup can cook longer, up to about 5 hours. Add the lemon juice shortly before serving.

Rainbow Soup

Yeast Free • Wheat/Gluten Free
Milk/Casein Free • Egg Free • Cholesterol Free
STAGE IV

A beautiful soup that tastes as good as it looks, **Rainbow Soup** is the perfect addition to any meal. For a 6-quart pot.

2 T. expeller pressed safflower oil

2 c. chopped leek

5 stalks celery, chopped coarsely

1 c. parsnips sliced into thin sticks

2 c. green bell pepper sliced into thin sticks

2 c. red bell pepper sliced into thin sticks

2 c. yellow bell pepper sliced into thin sticks

2 c. carrot sticks

2 c. cucumbers, peeled and cut into chunks

2 c. chopped tomatoes

1 T. dried basil

1-1/2 T. sea salt

12 c. water

Heat the oil in a 6 quart pot. When the oil is hot, **add ingredients in order**, sauteing after each addition until the latest addition is soft. For example, start with the leeks. Saute. When soft, add the celery. **Saute**. Then add the parsnips, then the peppers, then carrots, and so on. After all the vegetables are soft, **add** the basil, sea salt and water. Cover. Bring to a boil, then reduce to simmer. The soup is ready to eat in about 30 minutes, but cooking up to 2 hours brings out the best flavors.

Good for What Ails You Onion Soup

Yeast Free • Wheat/Gluten Free
Milk/Casein Free (without butter) • Egg Free • Cholesterol
Free (without butter)
STAGE IV

Our family clamors for this onion soup. The best part of all is
that it's so easy to make. Don't plan on a lot of leftovers! For
a light meal, serve with a salad and herbed brown rice. Or,
use this as the first course of a hearty meal on a cold winter
night. Or, just serve this whenever you need a pick me up.

    2 T. expeller pressed safflower oil or butter
    8 c. sliced or chopped mixed onions
        use: white bulb onions, leeks, scallions and some
        red onions for a really nice flavor
    4 cloves garlic, chopped
    1 T. sea salt, or salt to taste
    14 c. water

Heat the butter or oil in a 6 quart soup pot. When the butter
or oil is hot, **add** the onions and garlic. **Saute** until the
onions are golden brown and start to form their own sauce.
Add the salt while the onions are cooking. Add the water.
Cover. Bring to a boil; reduce to a **simmer**. Cook at least 30
minutes up to 2 hours. Serve hot.

Hidden Vegetable and Lentil Soup

Yeast Free • Wheat/Gluten Free
Milk/Casein Free • Egg Free • Cholesterol Free
STAGE IV

This soup gets its name from its appearance. The vegetables just disappear into the soup.

> 2 T. expeller pressed safflower oil
>
> 3-1/2 c. chopped white bulb onions or leeks
>
> 2 c. chopped celery
>
> 4 c. sliced zucchini
>
> 1/2 c. chopped carrots
>
> 1/2 c. chopped red pepper
>
> 2 c. chopped green beans
>
> 1 eggplant, peeled and cubed
>
> 1 T. sea salt
>
> 1 tsp. celery seed
>
> 1 tsp. dill seed
>
> 1 tsp. dried thyme
>
> 2 T. freshly squeezed lemon juice
>
> 1/2 c. brown rice
>
> 1/2 c. lentils
>
> 8 c. water

Heat the oil in a 6 quart soup pot. **Add** the onions; saute until they start to get soft. **Add remaining vegetables** (except eggplant) in order, **sauteing** after each addition. the celery; saute. After the vegetables are soft, **add** the eggplant. Saute until the eggplant is soft. Add the salt, herbs, lemon juice, rice and lentils. Add the water. **Cover**. Bring to a boil; reduce to **simmer**. Cook at least one hour, up to several hours for the best flavor.

Lemon Grass Vegetable Soup

Yeast Free • Wheat/Gluten Free
Milk/Casein Free • Egg Free • Cholesterol Free
STAGE IV

Lemon grass, available in Asian grocery stores and sometimes in produce markets, is an herb used in Thai and Vietnamese cooking. It imparts a lemony flavor to food not as sharp as fresh lemons. Lemon grass is tough and generally not eaten. If you want to remove the lemon grass before eating the soup, cook the lemon grass wrapped in cheese cloth and remove just before serving.

    2 stalks lemon grass
    2 T. expeller pressed safflower oil
    2-1/2 c. diagonally sliced celery
    1 heaping cup chopped scallions
    2 c. carrots, sliced in thin 1-1/2 inch matchsticks
    1-1/2 c. raw long-grain brown rice
    4 c. chopped tomato
    15 c. water
    1-1/2 T. sea salt

Prepare the lemon grass by removing the tough outer hull, slicing off the tough end, and slicing vertically down the center. Cut into 1-1/2 inch lengths. If desired, wrap in cheesecloth. Tie the end of the cheesecloth, or sew it. **Heat the oil** in a 6 quart pot. When the oil is hot, add the celery. **Saute** a few minutes. **Add** the scallions and carrots. **Saute** until the carrots are soft. Add the rice and **brown** it. When the rice is browned and vegetables are soft, **add** the tomatoes, lemon grass, water and salt. Cover. Bring to a **boil**; reduce to a **simmer**. Simmer until the rice is cooked, about an hour. Remove lemon grass, if desired. Adjust salt.

Chinese Tomato Soup

Yeast Free • Wheat/Gluten Free
Milk/Casein Free • Egg Free • Cholesterol Free
STAGE IV

This soup is so simple, yet so good, that you'll want to serve it again and again. If you like eggs, you can add some to make an egg drop soup. This recipe is based on a recipe in my favorite Chinese cookbook.

> 3 T. expeller pressed safflower oil
>
> 1 bunch scallions, chopped (about 1 heaping c.)
>
> 10 medium tomatoes, peeled (about 5 c.)
>
> 1 tsp. sea salt, plus more to taste
>
> 6 c. water
>
> 1-2 eggs (optional)
>
> 1 scallion, chopped (optional)
>
> 2 T. chopped fresh parsley (optional)

Heat the oil in a 3 quart pot. **Add** the scallions. Saute until the scallions start to get soft. **Core** the tomatoes and chop into large pieces. They will fall apart in the cooking. **Add** the tomatoes and **saute** for a few minutes. Add the salt. Stir. Add the water. Bring to a **boil**; reduce to **simmer**. Cook about 20 minutes. **For egg drop soup: Beat** the eggs in a small bowl. Use one "jumbo" or "extra large" egg, or 2 large size eggs. Bring the soup to a boil. When the soup is **boiling, pour** the eggs into the soup, stirring constantly. The eggs will cook in a few minutes. **Serve** immediately. If desired, add a few chopped scallions or some fresh parsley for a garnish.

Another Great Vegetable Soup #1

Yeast Free • Wheat/Gluten Free
Milk/Casein Free • Egg Free • Cholesterol Free
STAGE IV

Vegetable soups can be made with any vegetables you find in the refrigerator, and combinations of herbs that lend flavor to those vegetables. We have made so many different vegetable soups that we ran out of titles. The basic cooking instructions are to heat the oil, add vegetables one at a time and saute after each addition. Do not skip this step! The little oil you use multiplies the flavor of the soup many times. Add the herbs, salt and water; bring to a boil; reduce to a simmer and cook for an hour to several hours.

>   2 T. expeller pressed safflower oil
>
>   2 leeks, chopped
>
>   1 cauliflower, broken into florets
>
>   2 c. baby carrots
>
>   1 large cucumber, peeled and chopped
>
>   2 large tomatoes, chopped
>
>   1 tsp. each dried basil, thyme, oregano, marjorarm, tarragon and dill
>
>   1 bay leaf
>
>   1/8 tsp. dried sage
>
>   1 T. sea salt, or sea salt to taste
>
>   water to fill the pot to within 1 inch of the top

Heat the oil in a 6 quart pot. When the oil is hot, **add** the leeks. **Saute** until soft. **Add** the cauliflower and carrots. **Saute** until the cauliflower gets browned. **Add** the cucumber, tomatoes, herbs and salt. **Mix**. **Add water** to within 1 inch of the top of the pot. Cover. Bring to a **boil**. Reduce to a **simmer**. **Cook** for one hour to several hours.

Another Great Vegetable Soup #2

Yeast Free • Wheat/Gluten Free
Milk/Casein Free • Egg Free • Cholesterol Free
STAGE IV

2 T. expeller pressed safflower oil

1 leek, chopped

1 spring onion, chopped

1 clove elephant garlic, chopped

1 cubanel pepper, minced

4 c. chopped celery

4 c. whole baby carrots

5 small zucchini, sliced

1 T. sea salt

1 T. dried basil

4 medium red potatoes, peeled and cubed

1 bunch parsley, chopped

10-14 c. water

Heat the oil in a 6 quart pot. When the oil is hot, **add** the leek and onion. **Saute** until browned. **Add** garlic, peppers, celery, carrots and zucchini. **Saute** until the celery is soft. **Add** the salt, basil, parsley and potatoes. **Saute** a few minutes. **Add** water to within one inch of the top of the pot. Cover. Bring to a **boil**. Reduce to **simmer**. Cook at least one hour, up to about 5 hours.

Another Great Vegetable Soup #3

Yeast Free • Wheat/Gluten Free
Milk/Casein Free • Egg Free • Cholesterol Free
STAGE IV

2 T. expeller pressed safflower oil

2 large leeks, chopped

5 stalks celery, chopped

4 zucchini, peeled and sliced

3 parsnips, peeled and sliced

2 large carrots, peeled and sliced

1 cucumber, peeled and sliced

3 medium red or white potatoes, peeled and cubed

5 plum tomatoes

1 tsp. dried marjoram

1 tsp. dried tarragon

1 tsp. dried basil

1 tsp. dill seed

1 T. sea salt

water

Heat the oil in a 6 quart pot. When hot, **add** the leeks and celery. **Saute** until celery is soft. **Add** zucchini, parsnips, carrot. **Saute** a few more minutes. **Add** the cucumbers, potatoes, tomatoes, herbs and salt. **Mix** through. **Add** the water to within 1 inch of the top of the pot. Cover. Bring to a **boil**. Reduce to a **simmer**. **Cook** at least 2 hours. This soup can cook overnight if desired.

Vegetable Split Pea Soup

Yeast Free • Wheat/Gluten Free
Milk/Casein Free • Egg Free • Cholesterol Free
STAGE IV

2 T. expeller pressed safflower oil

5-6 scallions, chopped

1/3 c. chopped Cubanel pepper, or other mild chili pepper

5 stalks celery, chopped

4 medium zucchini, sliced

2 c. chopped green beans

1 c. dry split peas

1/2 c. dry baby lima beans

1-2 T. sea salt

2 tsp. dried basil

1 tsp. dried thyme

4 medium red potatoes, peeled and cubed

water

Heat the oil in a 6 quart pot. When hot, **add** the scallions and pepper. **Saute** until the scallions start to brown. **Add** the celery. Continue to **saute** until the celery starts to get soft. **Add** the zucchini and green beans. **Saute** until the green beans start to get soft. **Add** the split peas, lima beans, salt, basil, thyme and potatoes. **Saute** a few more minutes. **Add** water to within one inch of the top of the pot. **Cover**. Bring to a **boil**. Reduce to a **simmer**. **Cook** at least 4 hours, until the beans and peas are thoroughly cooked.

Red Rice Soup

Yeast Free • Wheat/Gluten Free
Milk/Casein Free • Egg Free • Cholesterol Free
STAGE IV

If you're ever in the mood for something really different, try this **Red Rice Soup**. Red rice is a type of wild rice that is very nutty in flavor and fluffy in texture. You can get red rice at natural food stores and cooperatives. Start this soup early in the day.

2 T. expeller pressed safflower oil
5 white bulb onions, chopped
   or 3 leeks, chopped
6 zucchini, sliced
5 stalks celery, chopped (including tops)
1 c. dry baby lima beans
1/2 c. Himalayan or Weihani red rice
1 tsp. dried basil
1 T. sea salt
water

Heat the oil in a 6 quart pot. When hot, **add** the onions or leeks. **Saute** until the onions are soft. **Add** the zucchini and celery. **Saute** until celery is soft. **Add** the beans, rice, basil and salt. **Saute** another minute or two. **Add** water to within 1 inch of the top of the pot. **Cover**. Bring to a **boil**. Reduce to a **high simmer/low boil**. **Cook** for at least 2 hours, until the beans and rice are very soft and the beans are falling apart.

Another Great Red Rice Soup

Yeast Free • Wheat/Gluten Free
Milk/Casein Free • Egg Free • Cholesterol Free
STAGE IV

2 T. expeller pressed safflower oil
2 white bulb onions, chopped
or 1 large leek, chopped
7 stalks celery, with tops, chopped
2 large zucchini, sliced
5 medium carrots, peeled and sliced
4 parsnips, peeled and sliced
1 c. chopped red bell pepper
1 c. red Weihani rice
1 T. dried basil
1 large or 2 small bay leaves
1 tsp. dill seed
1-1/2 T. sea salt
12-14 c. water

Heat the oil in a 6 quart pot. When hot, **add** the onions or leeks and celery. **Saute** until the onions and celery start to get soft. **Add** the zucchini, carrots and parsnips. **Saute** until the carrots start to get soft. **Add** the bell pepper, rice, basil, bay leaves, dill seed and salt. **Saute** a few minutes longer. **Add** the water. This should be enough water to come within an inch of the top of the pot. Cover. Bring to a boil. Reduce to a simmer. Cook at least one hour, until the rice is open and fluffy.

Asparagus Cauliflower Soup

Yeast Free • Wheat/Gluten Free
Milk/Casein Free • Egg Free • Cholesterol Free
STAGE IV

This soup is for lovers of asparagus and cauliflower only. But oh, boy, is it great!

3 T. expeller pressed safflower oil

1 large leek, chopped

1 lb. asparagus, cut into 1 inch pieces

4-5 c. cauliflower pieces

2 c. chopped red bell pepper

4 medium red potatoes, cubed

2 tsp. dried rosemary leaves, crushed

1-2 T. sea salt

water

Heat the oil in a 6 quart pot. When the oil is hot, **add** the leek. **Saute** until the leek is soft. **Add** the asparagus, cauliflower and pepper. **Saute** until the cauliflower is browned. **Add** the potatoes and saute a few more minutes. **Add** the rosemary and sea salt. **Add** water to within one inch of the top of the pot. **Cover**. Bring to a **boil**. Reduce to a **simmer**. Cook for at least two hours. Puree, if desired. However, the color will be a little brown.

Zucchini and Carrot Soup

Yeast Free • Wheat/Gluten Free
Milk/Casein Free • Egg Free • Cholesterol Free
STAGE IV

This is an easy, chunky vegetable soup that tastes delicious.

2 T. expeller pressed safflower oil
1/2 c. chopped leek
3-4 c. chunky chopped carrots
4 c. thickly sliced zucchini
2 tsp. dried basil
1 tsp. dried rosemary leaves, crushed
1 T. sea salt
4 c. cubed potatoes into 1/2 to 3/4 inch cubes
water

Heat the oil in a 6 quart pot. When hot, **add** the leeks. **Saute** until they start to get soft. **Add** the carrots and zucchini. **Saute** until the carrots start to get soft. **Add** the herbs and salt. **Add** the potatoes. **Saute** a few minutes. **Add** water to within an inch of the top of the pot. **Cover**. Bring to a **boil**. Reduce to a **simmer**. **Cook** for 1-2 hours. Serve hot.

Cholents

Cholent, an eastern European dish customarily served on the Jewish Sabbath, is an enticing mixture of grains, beans, vegetables, potatoes and sometimes meat The cholent cooks in a slow cooker for up to 24 hours before serving. It is irresistable on a cold winter day. All of the recipes that follow are favorite bean and rice cholent recipes. Cholent can be made with any combination of foods, however. Every family seems to have its own recipe, and in our synagogue, where we all participate in cooking a weekly Sabbath lunch, or Kiddush, we enjoy different flavors of cholent as well. The recipes in this book are my home recipes that I have converted to larger quantities. They are some of the favorites in our synagogue, or "shul," and in our home. I have received countless requests to "write them down." The "shul cholents" make enough cholent for a large crowd, about 120 people.   The home cholent is a large slow-cooker full. But you don't have to be Jewish to enjoy cholent. Try this any time you want something easy and delicious.

Sweet Shul Cholent

Yeast Free • Wheat/Gluten Free
Milk/Casein Free • Egg Free • Cholesterol Free
STAGE IV

For one 18-quart slow cooker, or three 6-quart slow cookers.

    2 c. dried kidney beans
    1 c. dried lentils
    1 c. dried black-eyed peas
    1 c. dried pinto beans

Sweet Shul Cholent, continued. . .

1 c. dried navy beans or baby lima beans
2 lb. long grained brown rice
1 c. short grain brown rice, or red rice
water
expeller pressed safflower oil
3 large red onions, chopped
7 cloves garlic, chopped
2 large brown or white onions, chopped
2 lb. carrots, peeled and chopped
1 bunch celery, chopped
5 lb. red or white potatoes, peeled and cubed
1 large yam or sweet potato, peeled and cubed
5 T. sea salt
water

In a large pot, **place** the beans and rice and about twice the amount of water as the beans and rice. Bring to a **boil**. Stir occasionally to prevent sticking. While the beans and rice are cooking, **heat the oil** in large frying pan. When hot, **add** the onions and garlic. **Saute** a few minutes. Add the carrots and celery. Saute until the carrots start to get soft. **Add** the potatoes. Saute until the potatoes start to get soft. Meanwhile, the beans and rice partially cook. **Combine** the sauteed vegetables with the partially cooked beans and rice in the slow cooker. **Add** the salt. Add water to within 2 inches of the top. Plug in and **cook** on medium-high for at least 12 hours, at most 24 hours. Eat!

Savory Shul Cholent

Yeast Free • Wheat/Gluten Free
Milk/Casein Free • Egg Free • Cholesterol Free
STAGE IV

This cholent also serves a crowd and is designed for one 18 quart slow cooker, or three 6-quart slow cookers. It is picante rather than sweet, but equally popular.

2 c. dried kidney beans

1 c. dried lentils

1 c. dried black-eyed peas

1 c. dried pinto beans

1 c. dried navy beans or baby lima beans

2 lb. long grained brown rice

1 c. short grain brown rice, or red rice

water

expeller pressed safflower oil

6 large white or brown onions, chopped

12 cloves garlic, chopped

2 lb. carrots, peeled and chopped

1 bunch celery, chopped

5 lb. red or white potatoes, peeled and cubed

5 T. sea salt

water

In a large pot, **place the beans** and rice and about twice the amount of water as the beans and rice. Bring to a **boil.** Stir occasionally to prevent sticking. While the beans and rice are cooking, **heat the oil** in large frying pan. When hot, add the onions and garlic. **Saute** a few minutes. Add the carrots and celery. **Saute** until the carrots start to get soft. **Add** the potatoes. **Saute** until the potatoes start to get soft. Meanwhile, the beans and rice partially cook. **Combine** the sauteed vegetables with the beans and rice in the slow cooker. Add the salt. Add water to within 2 inches of the top. **Plug in** and cook on medium-high for at least 12 hours, at most 24 hours. Eat!

Quick Cholent for the Family

Yeast Free • Wheat/Gluten Free
Milk/Casein Free • Egg Free • Cholesterol Free
STAGE IV

This is the cholent recipe I make most weeks, which my family devours over Saturday and Sunday, breakfast, lunch and dinner. It takes only a few minutes to put together.

For a 6 quart slow cooker:

1 c. dried baby lima beans

1 c. dried beans, including pintos or kidney beans, lentils, split peas, black-eyed peas, or garbanzo beans

2/3 c. long grained brown rice

2/3 c. red rice

4 medium red potatoes, peeled and cubed

1-1/2 T. sea salt

Water

Mix all ingredients in the slow cooker, except water. **Add** enough water to come to within 1 inch of the top. Plug in. **Cook** on medium high at least 12 hours. Overnight is better! Serve.

Quick Sweet Cholent for the Family

Yeast Free • Wheat/Gluten Free
Milk/Casein Free • Egg Free • Cholesterol Free
STAGE IV

This cholent is enough for a family, or a family with company. Similarly delicious, you don't need to invite the entire community to share it with you. This does not require advance cooking or sauteing. Generally, you can throw everything together on Friday afternoon and it will be cooked by Saturday lunch. Recipe is for a 6 quart slow cooker.

1 c. dried baby lima or navy beans

1 c. dried mixed beans, including pinto beans, lentils, kidney beans, split peas, and other beans

2/3 c. long grain brown rice

2/3 c. short grain brown rice

1 yam or sweet potato, peeled and cubed

3 medium red potatoes, peeled and cubed

1 red onion, chopped

2 cloves garlic, chopped

2 carrots, peeled and chopped

1 stalk celery, chopped

1-1/2 T. sea salt

Water

Mix all ingredients together in a 6 quart slow cooker, except the water. **Add** enough water to come to within 1 inch of the top. **Plug in and cook** on medium high at least 12 hours.

Lamb and Lentil Soup

Yeast Free • Wheat/Gluten Free
Milk/Casein Free • Egg Free
STAGE IV

2 T. expeller pressed safflower oil

2 leeks, chopped

2.5 lb. lamb stew meat, with bones

6 stalks celery, including tops, chopped

4 cloves garlic, chopped

3 zucchini, sliced

3 c. baby carrots

4 medium red potatoes, peeled and cubed

2 bay leaves

2 T. sea salt

2 T. fresh sage, chopped
    or 2 tsp. dried sage

1 tsp. dried rosemary

1 heaping tsp. dried thyme

2-3 c. brown lentils

water

Heat the oil in a 6 quart pot. **Add** the leek and onion. **Saute** until browned. **Add** the lamb and **saute** until the lamb is browned. **Add** celery, garlic, zucchini, carrots and potatoes. Continue sauteing. When celery starts to get soft, **add** the herbs and salt. Add the lentils. Add water to within an inch of the top of the pot. Cover. Bring to a **boil**. Reduce to **simmer**. **Cook** at least 2 hours. Serve hot.

Chicken Soup

Yeast Free • Wheat/Gluten Free
Milk/Casein Free • Egg Free
STAGE IV

Chicken Soup is good for whatever ails you, from colds to just wanting that home-made-great feeling. I have been asked often enough for my recipe that I included it in this book.   This recipe is for a 6 quart pot.

1 whole chicken, about 3 lb.

2 large leeks or white bulb onions, chopped coarsely

1/2 bunch celery, including tops, chopped coarsely

3 large carrots, peeled and chopped

3 large parsnips, peeled and chopped

1 tsp. dried basil

1 tsp. dried marjoram

1 tsp. dried thyme

1/2 tsp. ground sage

1/2 tsp.celery seed

1/4 tsp. black pepper

water

Wash the chicken thoroughly and remove any innards packed in the middle. **Pull off** any visible chunks of fat. Put the chicken, giblets, heart and neck in a 6 quart pot. Put the remaining ingredients in the pot. **Fill** the pot with water to within an inch of the top. Cover. Bring to a full **boil**. Reduce to a **fast simmer/slow boil**. After an hour, **test** the soup by sticking a large spoon into the chicken's body cavity. The soup is done when you lift the spoon and the chicken falls apart. Cook longer if desired, adding water when necessary.

Thanksgiving Friday Soup

Yeast Free • Wheat/Gluten Free
Milk/Casein Free • Egg Free • Cholesterol Free
STAGE IV

Ever wonder what to do with that leftover turkey on Thanksgiving? Not really the turkey--the turkey bones. This is our version of the traditional turkey carcass soup.

1 turkey carcass
water
1 lb. carrots
2 leeks, chopped
1 bunch celery
1-1/2 T. sea salt
1/2 tsp. dried marjoram
1 tsp. dried basil
1/2 tsp. dried thyme
1/2 tsp. celery seed
1/2 tsp. sage
Leftover rice stuffing

Fill a large pot (at least 8 quarts) half full of water. **Place** the turkey carcass in the pot and start to heat it. **Peel and chop** the carrots in large chunks. Add them to the pot. **Chop** the leeks and celery; add them to the pot. **Add** the salt and herbs. Add leftover rice stuffing (any type) if you desire. **Fill** with water to about one inch from the top of the pot. Bring to a **boil**. Reduce to **simmer**. Cook at least 20 minutes before devouring. This is best cooked longer, even overnight.

Veal Soup

Yeast Free • Wheat/Gluten Free
Milk/Casein Free • Egg Free
STAGE IV

This is a traditional bone soup, using veal neck bones. It should be started a day before you want to serve it, to allow the soup to cook overnight.

> 1-1/2 lb. veal neck bones
> 4 c. chopped celery
> 1-2 c. chopped carrots
> 1 leek, chopped
> 4 med. zucchini, chopped
> 1 c. red rice **or** brown rice
> 1 c. dried baby lima beans
> 1/2 c. lentils
> 3 T. sea salt
> 1 bay leaf
> 1/2 tsp. ground sage
> 1-1/2 tsp. dill seed
> 1 tsp. celery seed
> 1/2 red onion, chopped
> 1 clove elephant garlic, cut into chunks
> 1 tsp. marjoram
> water

Combine all ingredients in a 6-8 quart pot. The water should come to within an inch of the top of the pot. Cover. Bring to a **boil**. Reduce to a **simmer**. **Cook** several hours. This soup tastes best if you allow it to **cook at least 24 hours**.

Turkey Tomato Broth

Yeast Free • Wheat/Gluten Free
Milk/Casein Free • Egg Free
STAGE IV

Don't toss that turkey carcass! Make a delicious soup out of it. This broth is lighter and quicker than a traditional turkey soup, taking only a few minutes to put together. Start it right after you carve the turkey. Then let it cook overnight. This soup can simmer up to 24 hours for the fullest flavors. This tastes especially good with a few spoonfuls of leftover rice in it.

> 1 turkey carcass
>
> 1 T. sea salt or more to taste
>
> 4 large tomatoes, chopped
>
> 2 bulb onions, chopped in large pieces
>
> or equivalent amount of chopped leeks (about 2 cups)
>
> 1 T. dried oregano
>
> 1/2 T. dried marjoram
>
> 1/2 T. dried thyme
>
> water

Combine all ingredients in a large stock pot. **Fill** nearly to the top with water. **Cover.** Bring to a **boil**. Reduce to a quick **simmer** (almost boiling). **Simmer** for several hours. The bones and tomato skins will sink to the bottom of the pot. **Taste** periodically. Add salt if necessary. Check for sufficient water. After you like the soup's flavor, either skim the soup from the top or strain the broth to remove the bones and tomato skins. **Serve hot**.

Salads, Salad Dressings, Dips & Sauces

A salad is perfect for any occasion, from a light meal all alone to the centerpiece of a luncheon, to the beginning of a banquet. In this chapter, you will find more incredible mixed salads, several new salad dressings, and dips and sauces, including mayonnaise, salsa and other favorites!

☆   Salads

☆   Salad Dressings

☆   Dips & Sauces

Cucumber Pickle Salad

Yeast Free • Wheat/Gluten Free
Milk/Casein Free • Egg Free • Cholesterol Free
STAGE IV

Pickles, pickles and more pickles! Unfortunately, regular pickles are off limits on a yeast free diet. However, this salad, made from small pickling cucumbers, is so delicious that it will help you forget that you ever wanted "regular" pickles.

> 6 c. unpeeled, thinly sliced pickling cucumbers
>
> 2 T. chopped fresh chives
>
> 2 T. chopped fresh dill (optional)
>
> 3 T. freshly squeezed lemon juice
>
> 2 T. expeller pressed safflower oil
>
> 1 tsp. sea salt

Mix all ingredients together. **Cover**. **Chill** at least 2 hours before serving. Serve cold!

Lemon Salad

Yeast Free • Wheat/Gluten Free
Milk/Casein Free • Egg Free • Cholesterol Free
STAGE IV

So light, so bright, this salad is a favorite for children and adults. We seldom have leftovers with this salad; in fact, my children argue over who gets the last leaf of lettuce! This salad is especially good when you're in a hurry.

For a 12 cup salad (3 quart bowl):

> 9 c. lettuce pieces of mixed types of lettuce
> Tomatoes, chopped
> 2 scallions, chopped
> Other salad vegetables
> Sea salt to taste (about 1 tsp.)
> 1 tsp. dried basil
> 1 T. expeller pressed safflower oil
> 2 T. freshly squeezed lemon juice

Fill the bowl with lettuce, tomatoes, scallions and other salad vegetables. **Sprinkle** with sea salt, to taste. **Sprinkle** the basil over the salad. Toss thoroughly. Just before serving, **add** the oil and lemon juice. Do not add them too early or the salad will wilt. **Toss** thoroughly. Serve.

Garbanzo Bean and Pepper Salad

Yeast Free • Wheat/Gluten Free
Milk/Casein Free • Egg Free • Cholesterol Free
STAGE IV

If you are looking for the perfect, easy, salad for a light meal, try this one. Just serve with brown rice and you have a complete meal.

4 c. cooked garbanzo beans

3 mixed bell peppers (red, yellow, green)

1 med. or 1/2 large cucumber

2 tomatoes

3 T. freshly squeezed lemon juice

1 T. fresh chopped basil leaves

or 1 tsp. dried basil

1 tsp. fresh chopped tarragon leaves

or 1/4 tsp. dried tarragon

1-1/2 tsp. sea salt

Chop the peppers into small pieces. **Peel and chop** the cucumber. **Chop** the tomatoes. **Mix** all ingredients together in a large bowl. **Refrigerate** for a few hours. **Test** for salt. Add more if necessary. **Serve** cold.

Asparagus Pasta Salad

Yeast Free • Wheat/Gluten Free
Milk/Casein Free • Egg Free • Cholesterol Free
STAGE IV

A beautiful salad, perfect for a summer luncheon or dinner.

> 1 lb. asparagus, cut into 1 inch pieces
> water
> 10 oz. rice pasta spirals, cooked according to package directions
> 2 tsp. sea salt
> 2 tsp. dried basil
> 2 tsp. dried dill
> 1 c. chopped tomato
> 1 c. chopped red bell pepper
> 1 c. chopped yellow or green bell pepper
> 2-3 T. expeller pressed safflower oil

Blanch the asparagus: put the asparagus pieces into a pot of boiling water. Cook for a few minutes, until the asparagus is just cooked. Drain off the water and plunge the asparagus into a bowl of ice water. Then **mix** the pasta together with the sea salt, basil, and dill. Mix well. **Add** the tomato, peppers and asparagus. Mix well. Finally, add the oil. **Mix** thoroughly. **Chill** for at least one hour to overnight to allow the flavors to blend.

Black Bean Salad

Yeast Free • Wheat/Gluten Free
Milk/Casein Free • Egg Free • Cholesterol Free
STAGE IV

Simple salads are the best. This is easy to make, very colorful and tasty.

> 2 c. dry black beans, cooked
> 2-4 T. expeller pressed safflower oil
> 1 c. chopped red onion
> 2 c. chopped tomatoes
> Sea salt to taste

Mix the beans with enough safflower oil to coat them, but not so much that they are swimming in oil. **Add** the onion, tomatoes and sea salt to taste. **Chill**. Serve cold.

Wilted Spinach Salad

Yeast Free • Wheat/Gluten Free
Milk/Casein Free • Egg Free • Cholesterol Free
STAGE IV

If you love spinach, this is the salad for you!

spinach leaves to fill a 3-quart salad bowl
1/3 c. expeller pressed safflower oil
1/4 c. packed fresh basil leaves
2 cloves garlic, chopped
1/2 c. freshly squeezed lemon juice
1/4 c. water
1/2 tsp. sea salt

Prepare the spinach by **washing** each leaf thoroughly, twice, to remove sand. Remove stems, if desired. Drain and set aside in your salad bowl. **Refrigerate**. **Heat** the oil in a wok or frying pan. When the oil is hot, but not smoky, **add** the basil leaves. **Saute** for about 30 seconds. **Remove** the basil and oil, leaving just a trace of oil in the wok or frying pan. **Pour** the basil and oil into a jar with a wide mouth. **Reduce the heat** so the garlic won't burn. **Add** the garlic. Roast until brown on all sides. **Scrape** the garlic and remaining oil into the basil and oil mixture. Add the lemon juice, water and sea salt. **Shake** well. Let the dressing **sit** for at least one hour to allow flavors to mingle. Do not refrigerate. If needed, **heat** the dressing in the microwave before pouring over spinach. The dressing should be very warm to hot, so it wilts the spinach. **Pour** over spinach a few minutes before serving. **Toss** well. Serve when the spinach has wilted.

Up North Potato Salad

Yeast Free • Wheat/Gluten Free
Milk/Casein Free • Egg Free • Cholesterol Free
STAGE IV

In Wisconsin, we go "up north" during the summer--to swim, fish, sail, bike, hike and relax. This potato salad has the flavor of "up north," fresh and fun.

5 medium red potatoes

1 cucumber, peeled and diced

1 c. grape or cherry tomatoes, cut in half

1/4 c. freshly squeezed lemon juice

1-1/2 tsp. sea salt, or to taste

3 scallions, chopped

2 tsp. dried basil

Bake the potatoes in a microwave, or if unavailable, boil the potatoes in their skins. **Cool** just enough to peel. **Peel**. While the potatoes are still warm, **cut** them into cubes. **Mix** in the rest of the ingredients. This salad tastes great warm or cold.

Asparagus Dill Potato Salad

Yeast Free • Wheat/Gluten Free
Milk/Casein Free • Egg Free • Cholesterol Free
STAGE IV

This outstanding salad is perfect for asparagus season. This is a make-ahead dish, requiring time for the potatoes to cool. It refrigerates well, and is a good dish to serve the next day.

3 lb. red potatoes

water for cooking potatoes

1 lb. asparagus

ice water for cooling asparagus

water for cooking asparagus

1 c. chopped red bell pepper

2 T. fresh dill

1 tsp. sea salt

2-3 T. expeller pressed safflower oil

Boil the potatoes whole in their skins. **Cool** completely in water. A good way to cool them is in the refrigerator overnight. When cool, **slip** the skins off. Sometimes running the potatoes under hot water helps. **Cut** into 1/2 inch cubes and set aside. Now prepare the rest of the salad. Put ice cubes and water into a bowl. **Cut** the asparagus into 1 inch lengths. Place in a pot with a small amount of water. **Boil** for about a minute, until just cooked; **remove** the asparagus and **throw** into the ice water. Add the cooled asparagus to the potatoes. Add the pepper, dill, and sea salt. **Mix** thoroughly. Add 2-3 T. safflower oil, just enough to coat the potatoes and vegetables. **Toss.** Chill and enjoy!

Salad with Fresh Herbs

Yeast Free • Wheat/Gluten Free
Milk/Casein Free • Egg Free • Cholesterol Free
STAGE IV

Treat yourself during the summer to a green salad mixed with fresh herbs. This is the best summer salad!

Lettuce, tomatoes, and other fresh salad vegetables for a 4-quart salad bowl

Handful of mixed fresh herbs of any kind, finely cut

for example, use basil, rosemary, dill, chives and tarragon

1/2 tsp. sea salt

2 T. expeller pressed safflower oil

Juice of one freshly squeezed lemon

Prepare a green salad in a 4-quart salad bowl. **Toss** the fresh herbs and salt through the salad. **Mix** the safflower oil through the salad. Just before serving, mix the lemon juice through the salad. Serve immediately.

Fresh Basil and Tomato Salad

Yeast Free • Wheat/Gluten Free
Milk/Casein Free • Egg Free • Cholesterol Free
STAGE IV

Whenever you can get fresh basil, consider this salad. The taste is divine, and it is one of the easiest salads to make.

10 large, very ripe tomatoes
1 c. chopped fresh basil leaves, packed
1 tsp. sea salt
3-4 T. expeller pressed safflower oil

Chop the tomatoes into bite-sized pieces. Put them in a glass serving bowl. **Mix** the basil through the tomatoes. **Mix** the salt through the salad. **Taste** for salt. Add more if you like. **Mix** the oil through the salad. **Chill** for at least an hour to let the flavors mingle. Serve cold.

Pepper and Cucumber Dressing

Yeast Free • Wheat/Gluten Free
Milk/Casein Free • Egg Free • Cholesterol Free
STAGE IV

For a really refreshing salad dressing, try this. It makes about 1 cup of dressing and freezes well.

1 heaping c. chopped, peeled cucumber

1/4 c. coarsely chopped cubanel pepper

1/3 c. expeller pressed safflower oil

1 tsp. sea salt

squeeze of fresh lemon juice

Combine all ingredients in a food processor. Process until smooth.

Basic Lemon Salad Dressing

Yeast Free • Wheat/Gluten Free
Milk/Casein Free • Egg Free • Cholesterol Free
STAGE IV

This is a passed around recipe to which our friend Joan Gertel introduced us. It is about as good and basic as you can get. This dressing goes well with every type of vegetable and can be made in a hurry.

1/2 c. freshly squeezed lemon juice

1/2 c. expeller pressed safflower oil

1 tsp. sea salt

Mix all ingredients together in a jar. **Shake** well. Chill and serve.

Roasted Garlic and Lemon Salad Dressing

Yeast Free • Wheat/Gluten Free
Milk/Casein Free • Egg Free • Cholesterol Free
STAGE IV

This simple and flavorful dressing is tangy and pungent without being overdone.

2 T. expeller pressed safflower oil

3 cloves garlic, peeled

juice of one
fresh lemon

1/2 tsp. sea
salt, plus
more to taste

Heat the oil in a small saucepan. When hot, **add** the garlic. **Brown**. Remove from heat. **Mash** the garlic in the oil. **Mix** in the lemon juice and sea salt. Add more sea salt, if desired, to taste. **Cool** the dressing. When totally cool, **pour** over a green salad. Toss and serve.

Joan's Red Onion Salad Dressing

Yeast Free • Wheat/Gluten Free
Milk/Casein Free • Egg Free • Cholesterol Free
STAGE IV

This recipe came to us from our friend Joan Gertel, who brought over one of the most delicious salad dressings we've tasted. We adapted the dressing to the 4 Stages diet, keeping the taste but leaving out the vinegar and sugar. This looks like bubble gum and tastes like a dream. This is great on green salads, cole slaws, and vegetables. Yield: about 1 cup. Keeps 3-4 days in the refrigerator, and freezes well.

1/2 c. expeller pressed safflower oil

1/3 c. freshly squeezed lemon juice

1/4-1/2 c. chopped bermuda (red) onion (if using older onions, use 1/2 c. If using "farmer's market fresh" onions, use 1/4 c.)

3 T. natural honey

1/2 tsp. sea salt

Puree all ingredients in a food processor until the onions are completely pureed. Chill and serve.

Creamy Cucumber Basil Dressing

Yeast Free • Wheat/Gluten Free
Milk/Casein Free • Egg Free • Cholesterol Free
STAGE IV

This cool creamy dressing is a variation on our ever popular **Creamy Cucumber Dressing,** from **Feast Without Yeast** (p. 101).

1 cucumber

1/3 c. expeller pressed safflower oil

1 tsp. dried basil

1 tsp. sea salt

1/2 to 1 tsp. freshly squeezed lemon juice

Peel and chop the cucumber into chunks. **Place** all ingredients in a blender. **Blend** on high for several minutes until the cucumber is completely pureed. **Chill**. Serve over green salad, or as a dressing for fish. Keeps in refrigerator about 3 days. Freezes well.

Sweet Red Pepper Dressing

Yeast Free • Wheat/Gluten Free
Milk/Casein Free • Egg Free • Cholesterol Free
STAGE IV

This salad dressing is simple and sweet. The scallions taste great, but have a tendency to turn the color slightly brown. If this bothers you, use the white onion instead.

1 c. chopped red bell pepper

1/3 c. expeller pressed safflower oil

1/2-1 tsp. sea salt

1/2 scallion, chopped

　or 1-2 T. chopped white bulb onion

1/4 tsp. dried thyme

2 squeezes fresh lemon

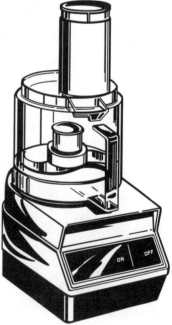

Put all ingredients in a food processor. Process until smooth. Makes about one cup.

Thousand Island Dressing

Yeast Free • Wheat/Gluten Free
Milk/Casein Free
STAGE IV

I love **Thousand Island Dressing**, but it traditionally is made with mayonnaise, ketchup and pickles, none of which is acceptable on a yeast free diet. This **Thousand Island Dressing** tastes even better than the traditional one, and is totally acceptable on a yeast free diet.

> 1/2 c. **Homemade Mayonnaise** (recipe on p. 83)
>
> 3/4 c. chopped tomato
>
> 2 tsp. natural honey
>
> 1/4 c. finely chopped green bell pepper

Put the **Homemade Mayonnaise**, tomato and honey in a food processor. Process until completely smooth. Remove from the food processor into a jar. Stir in the bell pepper. Chill. Makes about 1-1/4 cups.

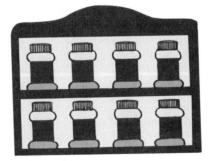

Italian Dressing

Yeast Free • Wheat/Gluten Free
Milk/Casein Free • Egg Free • Cholesterol Free
STAGE IV

Everyone loves a good, basic Italian-type dressing. This is good for salads, marinades, and whatever else you need.

1/2 c. freshly squeezed lemon juice
1/2 c. water
1/2 c. expeller pressed safflower oil
1 tsp. dried oregano
1 tsp. dried basil
1 tsp. sea salt

Combine all ingredients in a jar. **Shake** well. **Chill** for at least 45 minutes to 1 hour before serving.

Heavenly Salad Dressing

Yeast Free • Wheat/Gluten Free
Milk/Casein Free • Egg Free • Cholesterol Free
STAGE IV

One afternoon in the kitchen, our friend E'liane Khang and I were experimenting with salad dressings. This dressing is the result. It is called Heavenly because that is how it tastes. Try it and see for yourself.

1/4 c. white bulb onion, chopped

1/3 c. expeller pressed safflower oil

2-1/2 T. natural honey

4-1/2 T. freshly squeezed lemon juice

1 tsp. sea salt

1/4 c. water

1/2 tsp. dried thyme

Put all ingredients in a food processor. Process until smooth. Chill and serve!

Guacamole

Yeast Free • Wheat/Gluten Free
Milk/Casein Free • Egg Free • Cholesterol Free
STAGE IV

Quick, easy, delicious, and complements any meal.

> 2 medium or 1 large ripe avocado
> sea salt to taste
> 1/2 medium tomato, chopped
> squeeze of fresh lemon juice

Peel and mash the avocado. It should be very soft and ripe.
Mix the remaining ingredients through. Serve.

Homemade Mayonnaise

Yeast Free • Wheat/Gluten Free
Milk/Casein Free
STAGE IV

Homemade mayonnaise is creamy and delicious, a great addition to sandwiches, a dip for vegetables, or even a sauce for vegetables. It is lighter than regular mayonnaise and has a creamier consistency. Mayonnaise is an emulsion, a type of mixture in which the foods are combined by breaking each food into tiny particles. You need a food processor to do this properly. If you are very steady, you can try using a blender and pouring the oil in steadily. This recipe makes about 1-1/2 cups, and keeps in the refrigerator for up to a week.

> 1 egg
>
> 1/2 tsp. sea salt
>
> 3 T. freshly squeezed lemon juice
>
> 1 c. expeller pressed safflower oil

In the bottom of a food processor, put the egg, salt and lemon juice. **Process** until all ingredients are blended. Put the small feed tube (with the little hole at the bottom) in the feed tube slot. With the food processor going constantly, **pour oil** into the feed tube. It will steadily stream out of the hole at the bottom into the egg and lemon mixture. **Continue pouring oil** into the feed tube until all the oil is used. **Continue processing** until the mayonnaise is a creamy consistency. **Do not stop** the food processor until you reach this consistency!

Celery Seed Mayonnaise

Yeast Free • Wheat/Gluten Free
Milk/Casein Free
STAGE IV

When making homemade mayonnaise (page 83), add 1 tsp. celery seed to the egg, salt and lemon. Continue processing as before. Celery seed mayonnaise tastes great as an artichoke dip and with fish.

Basil Mayonnaise

Yeast Free • Wheat/Gluten Free
Milk/Casein Free
STAGE IV

When making homemade mayonnaise (page 83), add 1 tsp. dried basil to the egg, salt and lemon. Continue processing as before. Basil mayonnaise tastes great on just about everything.

Tahini Sauce

Yeast Free • Wheat/Gluten Free
Milk/Casein Free • Egg Free • Cholesterol Free
STAGE IV

When you're in the mood for something different, try this, a middle-eastern sesame sauce. Although usually served with **Falafel** page 110), **Tahini Sauce** also makes a delicious dip for vegetables.

1/2 c. sesame seeds

3 T. expeller pressed safflower oil

1/3 c. water

2 T. lemon juice

1/2 to 1 tsp. sea salt

2 T. chopped fresh parsley

Process the sesame seeds in food processor until pulverized, at least 5 minutes. **Add the oil** and continue to process, stopping every 30 seconds or so to scrape the sides of the bowl. **Slowly add** the water and lemon juice, continuing to process. This takes at least 5 minutes. **Process** until totally smooth.

Hot Salsa!

Yeast Free • Wheat/Gluten Free
Milk/Casein Free • Egg Free • Cholesterol Free
STAGE IV

This salsa is HOT! But great, especially with **Tacos**, page 108.

3 c. chopped tomatoes

1 c. chopped green bell pepper

2 T. minced fresh jalapeno pepper

(Hint: when mincing the pepper, wear disposable rubber gloves so the pepper juice does not get on your hands. Discard the gloves as soon as you are done chopping.)

2/3 c. chopped mild chili pepper, such as a Cubanel pepper

2 T. freshly squeezed lemon juice

2 T. expeller pressed safflower oil

1 tsp. sea salt

Mix all ingredients in a microwave safe glass bowl.
Cover with plastic wrap. **Microwave** on high 13-15 minutes. Allow to **cool** to room temperature. Then place in refrigerator to **chill**. Makes about 2 cups of salsa. Freezes well.

Lemony Light Cranberry Sauce

Yeast Free • Wheat/Gluten Free
Milk/Casein Free • Egg Free • Cholesterol Free
STAGE IV

This cranberry sauce relies more on pears and less on honey for sweetness. It is refreshing and tangy, and has fewer calories than our other cranberry sauces.

> 2-1/2 c. fresh cranberries (one standard package)
>
> 1 Bartlett pear, peeled and chopped
>
> 1/2 c. natural clover honey
>
> 1 lemon, sliced with peel on

Combine all ingredients. **Cook** on low heat until all the berries have burst and mixture is boiling. **Remove** from heat and **cool** slowly, uncovered. The sauce will thicken as it cools. Serve with turkey or potato latkes, or just eat plain.

Notes

Main Dishes

Whether you are looking for meat, vegetables, or beans to serve, or a surprising combination of all three, you will find lots of scrumptious recipes in this chapter! Don't forget about pasta as another main dish. For even more ideas, be sure to check out the chapter on **Pasta and Pasta Sauces**, starting on page 125.

☆   Mainly Meat

☆   Meat & Vegetarian

☆   Vegetarian

Veal Stuffing Casserole

Yeast Free • Wheat/Gluten Free
Milk/Casein Free • Egg Free
STAGE IV

This dish is perfect for Thanksgiving, but great anytime. It is so delectable that you'll have a hard time saving enough from nibblers to put into a casserole dish.

> 2 T. expeller pressed safflower oil
> 1 c. chopped celery
> 3 cloves garlic, chopped
> 2 lb. ground veal
> 1 tsp. dill seed
> 1/2 tsp. dried thyme
> 1/2 tsp. dried marjoram
> 1 tsp. dried sage
> 1 tsp. dried basil
> 3 c. cooked brown rice
> 1-1/2 tsp. sea salt

Preheat the oven to 350F. **Heat** the oil in a frying pan. **Add** the celery and garlic. **Saute** until the celery is soft. **Add** the ground veal. **Brown** the veal with the celery and garlic. Add herbs while the meat is cooking. When the meat is cooked, **add** the rice. Mix through. Add the salt. Pour into a casserole dish. Cover. **Bake** at 350F for 45 minutes.

Veal Meatloaf

Yeast Free • Wheat/Gluten Free
Milk/Casein Free • Egg Free
STAGE IV

When you think of meatloaf, you may think of dried school cafeteria fare. This meatloaf will make you retool your memories! Delicately seasoned and moist, you will be hard-pressed to save enough for leftover meatloaf sandwiches the next day. Try it!

>   2 lb. ground veal
>
>   1/2 tsp. dried basil
>
>   1/2 tsp. dried marjoram
>
>   1/4 tsp. dried sage
>
>   1/4 tsp. dried thyme
>
>   1 tsp. sea salt
>
>   expeller pressed safflower oil
>
>   4 red potatoes, peeled and cubed
>
>   2 carrots, peeled and chopped
>
>   1 large tomato, sliced

Mix the ground veal with the seasoning. **Lightly oil** a small pyrex baking dish or pie pan. **Form** the meat into loaf. Put the loaf into the oiled baking dish and turn it over, so the meatloaf is oiled all over. **Place** the loaf in the center of the baking dish. Place the cubed potatoes and chopped carrots around the loaf. Place tomato slices on the meatloaf and over the potatoes and carrots. **Cover** tightly with aluminum foil. **Bake** at 375 F. for one hour. **Remove** from oven and let sit at least 20 minutes for the flavors to be absorbed.

Chicken Fingers

Yeast Free • Wheat/Gluten Free
Milk/Casein Free • Egg Free
STAGE IV

Children love chicken fingers. These have no breading, so they are different from the commercial chicken fingers you might buy. They are fun to eat and make great snacks. Cook a batch, freeze, then take out and heat up what you need.

> Any amount boneless, skinless chicken breasts
> Expeller pressed safflower oil
> Sea salt to taste
> Dried basil to taste
> Dried oregano to taste

Preheat the oven to 375 F. **Lightly oil** two baking sheets. **Cut** the chicken into strips, about 1 inch wide and 2 inches long. Lay them out in a single layer on the cookie sheets. **Sprinkle** with sea salt, basil and oregano. **Bake**, uncovered, until cooked through, about 20 minutes. Serve hot, cold, or freeze and use later.

Roasted Veal

Yeast Free • Wheat/Gluten Free
Milk/Casein Free • Egg Free
STAGE IV

Every once in awhile, we love just a plain roast. Veal is a
tender, juicy meat that hits the spot.

expeller pressed safflower oil
1 bunch celery, including leaves
2 pounds carrots, peeled
2 large leeks
5-10 red potatoes, peeled and halved
1 red onion, chopped into 8 pieces
3 pound veal roast, wrapped with string
2 large cloves garlic, chopped
1 tsp. dried rosemary
1/8 tsp. dried thyme powder
1/8 tsp. dried sage powder
1 tsp. dried marjoram
sea salt to taste
5 medium tomatoes

Lightly oil a medium sized roasing pan with the safflower oil.
Preheat the oven to 350F. **Chop** the celery, carrots and leeks
into pieces about 2-3 inches long. **Spread** the potatoes,
carrots, celery and leeks in the roasting pan. **Nestle** the veal
roast among the vegetables. **Rub** the veal with garlic, and
place pieces of garlic under the string. **Spread** some of the
garlic over the vegetables. **Sprinkle** the herbs and salt over
the meat and vegetables. **Top** with sliced tomatoes. Cover.
Roast at 350F for about 2-1/2 hours.

Roasted Veal Shanks with Rice and Vegetables

Yeast Free • Wheat/Gluten Free
Milk/Casein Free • Egg Free
STAGE IV

This is a favorite way to make an all-inclusive meal. The main part of the meal really is the rice and vegetables. The veal adds its unique flavors and textures for a rich and satisfying meal. Serve with a salad or soup, and you have plenty!

3 c. long grain brown rice

6 c. water

1 T. sea salt or more, to taste

1/2 tsp. ground sage

1/2 tsp. ground thyme

2 c. cooked garbanzo beans

5 stalks celery, chopped

3-4 carrots, peeled and chopped

3 white bulb onions, chopped

1 clove elephant garlic, chopped

1 leek, chopped

5 red potatoes, peeled and cubed

2-1/2 to 3 lb. boneless veal shanks

Additional water, as needed

Preheat the oven to 350F. In a roasting pan, place the rice, water, salt and herbs. **Mix** well. Then **scatter** the beans and vegetables in the rice and water. **Lay** the veal shanks over the vegetables. **Roast** covered or uncovered for 3-1/2 hours, adding water as needed. You will need to add extra water if you bake this uncovered, but the veal shanks will be nicely browned. Serve hot.

Meatballs & Onions

Yeast Free • Wheat/Gluten Free
Milk/Casein Free • Egg Free
STAGE IV

This recipe started out as meatballs for a spaghetti sauce. However, the meatballs were just too good with the onions to mix into another sauce. Serve these plain or over pasta or rice.

2 lb. ground veal

1-2 tsp. sea salt (to taste)

1 tsp. oregano

4 T. expeller pressed safflower oil

2 white bulb onions, chopped

Mix veal with salt and oregano. **Pack** into meatballs 1-1/2 inch in diameter. Really **press** each meatball together so they hold together during cooking. **Heat** the safflower oil in a frying pan. When hot, **gently place** some meatballs in the frying pan. Then **put the onions** in the frying pan. You may not get all the meatballs in in one batch. Let the meatballs **cook** until the part on which they are sitting is well browned. Then gently **roll** them around to another area. **Repeat** until the meatballs are well-browned and cooked through. **Take out** the meatballs, but keep the onions in the pan. **Stir** around the onions. **Add** another batch of meatballs, and cook as before. **Repeat** the cooking process until all the meatballs are done. When you **remove** the last batch of meatballs, **pour** the onions and any gravy over the meatballs. **Stir** thoroughly. Serve hot over rice or rice pasta.

E'liane's Chinese Roast Duck

Yeast Free • Wheat/Gluten Free
Milk/Casein Free • Egg Free
STAGE IV

Duck is a treat, but this traditional Chinese version of roast duck makes your mouth water. We thank our friend E'liane Khang for this recipe. If you are using a duck that is not pre-salted and soaked, you must start this recipe the day before you want to serve it.

> 1 duck
> sea salt
> 2 start anise
> 2-3 slices fresh ginger root
> 3 whole scallions
> natural honey

If your duck is not pre-salted and soaked, **rub salt** on the duck, inside and out. Wrap in aluminum foil. **Soak** overnight in refrigerator. **Remove** the foil and rinse the duck. If using kosher or other pre-salted duck, start here. **Rinse** the duck thoroughly. **Place** inside the body cavity the anise, ginger and scallions. Place the duck on a **rack** in a roasting pan. **Roast**, uncovered, at 400F for 15-20 minutes, then reduce to 375F and roast for 45 minutes. **Remove** the duck from the oven. **Coat** the duck with honey. Replace in the oven. **Roast** for another 45 minutes to 75 minutes, until done.

Lemon Ginger Chicken

Yeast Free • Wheat/Gluten Free
Milk/Casein Free • Egg Free
STAGE IV

This exceptionally tasty chicken is made in a bag, and takes about 10 minutes to prepare!

2 T. rice flour

6 boneless chicken breasts

4 scallions, chopped

3 T. freshly squeezed lemon juiice

1 tsp. sea salt

1 tsp. or more fresh minced ginger root

Preheat oven to 350F. Put the rice flour in a plastic oven bag made for baking meat. **Shake** to coat the bag. Put all ingredients into the bag and **shake**. **Close** the bag with the manufacturer's twist-tie. **Slit** the bag, if manufacturer recommends it. **Bake** at 350F according to bag manufacturer's directions. When done, open the bag and place the chicken on a platter. Pour the juice from the bag over the chicken. **Cool** slightly, then serve.

Chicken & Vegetables

Yeast Free • Wheat/Gluten Free
Milk/Casein Free • Egg Free
STAGE IV

You can't beat this basic herbed, roasted chicken with vegetables for flavor and ease. It's a complete meal if you add rice, soup and a simple salad.

> 4 c. chopped celery
> 4 large carrots, chopped
> 1 leek, chopped
> 2 c. water
> 2 tsp. dried rosemary
> 2 tsp. dried thyme
> 1/2 tsp. ground sage
> 2 tsp. sea salt
> 5 lbs. cut up chicken

Preheat the oven to 375F. **Scatter** the vegetables on the bottom of a roasting pan. **Sprinkle** the salt and herbs over them. **Mix** them around. **Pour** water into the roaster. **Nestle** the chicken pieces among the vegetables, putting some vegetables on top of the chicken. **Roast** covered for wetter chicken, uncovered for drier chicken, at 375F for 60-90 minutes.

Roasted Chicken with Ginger and Peppers

Yeast Free • Wheat/Gluten Free
Milk/Casein Free • Egg Free
STAGE IV

Roasted chicken is never ordinary when you add this beautiful and diverse array of colors and flavors!

  expeller pressed safflower oil for greasing pan
  1 cut up fryer chicken, 3-4 lb.
  2-3 tsp. sea salt
  1 c. chopped white bulb onion
      or 1 c. chopped leek
  5 stalks celery, sliced
  1 clove elephant garlic, chopped
  4 colored bell peppers, sliced in strips (red, yellow, orange, etc.)
  5 scallions, chopped
  5 red potatoes, peeled and cubed
  4 tsp. chopped fresh ginger

Preheat the oven to 375F. **Lightly oil** a covered roasting pan. **Place** the chicken pieces in the pan. **Sprinkle liberally** with 2 tsp. sea salt. **Add** all the vegetables, garlic, potatoes and ginger, **spreading** them around the chicken. **Sprinkle** with the remaining teaspoon of sea salt. **Cover**. **Roast** at 375F for 90 minutes, or until all the vegetables and chicken are cooked.

Pot Roast

Yeast Free • Wheat/Gluten Free
Milk/Casein Free • Egg Free
STAGE IV

This extremely tasty, tender pot roast is a hit with children and adults alike.

> 1-4 lb. chuck roast, or Chicago roast, or other meat for pot roast
>
> 3 white onions, cut into eighths
>
> 1 red onion, cut into eighths
>
> 6 extra large carrots, peeled and chopped into large chunks
>
> 7 medium red potatotes, peeled and cut into fourths
>
> 7 cloves garlic, peeled
>
> 1 tsp. dried rosemary leaves, crushed
>
> 1 tsp. dried thyme
>
> 1 tsp. dill week
>
> 2 tsp. sea salt
>
> 3 large tomatoes, sliced

Preheat the oven to 350F. **Wash** the meat thoroughly. Take a large roasting pan. **Put the onions**, potatoes and carrots in the roasting pan. **Nestle** the meat among the vegetables, if the meat is tied with string. If not, lay the meat on some of the vegetables and place others over the meat. **Place** the garlic under the string or scatter directly on top of the meat. **Sprinkle** the herbs and salt over the meat and vegetables. Lay the tomato slices on top of the meat. **Cover**. **Roast** at 350F for 3-4 hours, until the meat is very tender. Serve over rice noodles or brown rice.

Chili Con Carne

Yeast Free • Wheat/Gluten Free
Milk/Casein Free • Egg Free
STAGE IV

This chili is so good you'll want to make it again and again. You control the "heat" by choosing the peppers --mild peppers for mild chili, hot peppers for hot chili. Try this on a cold winter day. You can serve this chili as a one pot meal, or you can make a meal of it with salad and rice.

1 c. dried kidney beans

1 clove elephant garlic, sliced in half

1/2 banana pepper, sliced in half

4 c. water

1 c. dry long grain brown rice

2 T. expeller pressed safflower oil

3 c. chopped red onions

2 lb. ground veal

3 tsp. minced chili pepper

  For mild chili, use Cubanel or other mild pepper

  For hot chili, use Banana pepper or other hot pepper

2 cloves minced garlic, about 2 tsp.

1 T. sea salt

1/4 tsp. ground black pepper

1 T. dried oregano

14 plum tomatoes, choppped

4 c. water

Prepare the beans: place the beans, elephant garlic, banana pepper and water in a pot. Bring to a boil. Turn off heat; let sit one hour. Bring to a boil again, reduce to simmer and cook one hour or until soft. Drain. Rinse. Set aside. **Prepare the rice**: put the dry rice in a food processor. Pulverize until the rice grains are about 1/4 their original size. Set aside. **Prepare the rest of the chili**: **Heat** the safflower oil in the bottom of a large kettle, about 6-8 quarts. When the oil is hot, **add** the chopped onions. Brown the onions. Then add the veal. **Brown**. **Add** the minced chili peppers and garlic. Cook until the peppers are soft. **Add** the beans to the veal and onion mixture, including the peppers and elephant garlic that was cooked with the beans. **Mix** well. Now **add the remaining ingredients**: pulverized rice, sea salt, black pepper, oregano, tomatoes and water. Mix well. Cover. Bring the entire mixture to a boil. Reduce to simmer. Cook at least two hours. Serve hot!

Cook's note: If you don't have time to prepare the beans, or if you have cooked kidney beans on hand, instead of cooking the beans with the elephant garlic and chili peppers, you can add the plain cooked beans to the chili and add the elephant garlic and sliced banana pepper directly to the chili. This does not taste quick as good as the other method, but it works.

Roast Turkey

Yeast Free • Wheat/Gluten Free
Milk/Casein Free • Egg Free
STAGE IV

This recipe is just a basic roasted turkey recipe. If you buy a great turkey, this is a great recipe. We always use Kosher turkeys, which are moist and tender.

> 1 whole turkey
>
> expeller pressed safflower oil
>
> sea salt

Preheat the oven to 325F. **Thoroughly clean** the turkey, inside and out. **Remove** any giblets. **Remove** the visible chunks of fat. **Stuff** the turkey with your choice of stuffing from this book or Feast Without Yeast. **Lightly oil** the turkey skin. **Lightly salt** the entire turkey. **If using a turkey bag,** follow manufacturer's directions for roasting. **If not using a turkey bag,** place the turkey breast side up in a roasting pan. Put in the oven at **325F. Roast for 20 minutes per pound** for a stuffed turkey. **Do not baste.** The turkey skin should be golden brown and the leg should move easily when the turkey is done. If in doubt, use a meat thermometer to check. **Remove** the turkey from the oven. Let the turkey **sit at least 20 minutes** before carving to allow the juices to soak into the meat. Remove the stuffing and place it in an oven proof bowl. **Carve** the turkey, laying out the pieces on a serving tray or in a pyrex baking pan. As you carve the turkey, **dip** the slices in the turkey gravy in the pan or spoon some gravy over the slices. This keeps the turkey extra moist. **Cover** with foil. Cover the stuffing. Place both in a 200F oven until ready to serve.

Basic Microwaved Fish Fillets

Yeast Free • Wheat/Gluten Free
Milk/Casein Free • Egg Free
STAGE IV

Even frozen fish fillets can be exciting. They make a quick high-protein meal every once in awhile.

> 4 frozen fish fillets, Cod or Tilapia or similar fish
> juice of 1/2 lemon
> 1/2 tsp. sea salt
> 1/2 tsp. dried dill

Place the frozen fish fillets in a covered glass baking dish. **Squeeze** the lemon juice over the fish. **Sprinkle** the salt and dill over the fish. **Cover.** **Place** in the microwave oven. If your microwave has a sensor, press "fish fillets." If not, **microwave** on high for about 2 minutes per fillet. Test to see if done. The fish is done when it flakes easily. If the fish is not done, cover and microwave until done. Serve hot.

Stuffed Cabbage

Yeast Free • Wheat/Gluten Free
Milk/Casein Free • Egg Free
STAGE IV

Stuffed cabbage is the perfect "fancy" meal. It looks beautiful, is relatively easy to make (although time consuming), and of course tastes wonderful. We make half with meat and half with rice filling, to satisfy all tastes. This makes about 12-13 good sized veal rolls and a similar number of rice rolls.

Cabbage:
3 small, 2 medium or 1 large cabbage

Prepare by placing the cabbage in a plastic bag, sealing the bag, and putting in the microwave for about 25 minutes. While the cabbage is cooling, prepare the sauce and the fillings.

Sauce:
2 T. expeller pressed safflower oil
2 large red bell peppers, chopped (about 2 cups)
2 tsp. dried dill
2 tsp. dried marjoram
2 tsp. sea salt
10 plum tomatoes, chopped
3 T. natural honey
1 T. freshly squeezed lemon juice

Heat the oil in a skillet. When hot, add the peppers. Saute until soft. Add the herbs, salt and tomatoes. Cover. Cook. While the sauce is cooking, make the fillings.

Veal Filling:

2 lb. ground veal

1 tsp. sea salt

1 tsp. dried marjoram

1 tsp. dried dill

Mix the meat with the seasonings. Set aside.

Rice filling:

2 c. cooked brown rice

1/2 tsp. dried basil

1/2 tsp. dried marjoram

1/2 tsp. dried dill

1 tsp. sea salt

up to 1 c. beans, if desired

Mix all ingredients together. Set aside.

Now you are ready to **assemble** the stuffed cabbage. Preheat the oven to 375 F. Carefully **core** the cooled cabbage. **Separate** each leaf and lay on a plate. Try not to tear too many. After the leaves are separated, put some **filling** (either meat or rice) in the middle of the leaf. **Fold** the ends over and roll. **Put some sauce** on the bottom of a 9x13 inch pyrex pan. **Place** the cabbage roll smooth side up (open side down) in the sauce. **Continue filling** the cabbage rolls and placing them in a single layer in the pan. Usually you need a second baking pan. When the filling is all used up, you are done rolling! If you have extra cabbage, just eat it. It's surprisingly good. Now **pour** the sauce over the cabbage rolls, dividing evenly between your pans. **Bake** uncovered at 375 F. for one hour. Serve hot.

Tacos

Yeast Free • Wheat/Gluten Free
Milk/Casein Free • Egg Free • Cholesterol Free (without meat)
STAGE IV

For real south of the border flavor, try these tacos. Make the filling (or fillings), the sauce, and use purchased corn taco shells (if permissible), and/or make **Rice Flatbread** (recipe on page 143). Serve by placing the fillings, sauce and shells/ flatbread on the table. Also place a bowl of shredded lettuce and another bowl of chopped tomatoes on the table. If you can eat cheese, or soy or rice cheese, grate some cheese for an extra garnish. Let each person create their own taco, using whatever fillings and garnishes they like!

Taco Bean Filling

2 T. expeller-pressed safflower oil

2 scallions, chopped (about 1/2 c.)

1 tsp. dried oregano

2 tsp. sea salt

1 c. chopped tomatoes

5 c. cooked pinto beans (about 2 c. dried pinto beans, cooked)

Heat frying pan until hot. Add safflower oil. When the oil is hot, add the scallions. **Saute.** When scallions are soft, add the tomatoes and salt. **Cook down** until the tomatoes start to form a sauce, but are still chunky. **Add** the beans. Cook, stirring well, until the beans start to break apart and are soft. **Set aside** for filling.

Taco Veal Filling

1-2 T. expeller pressed safflower oil

1 lb. ground veal

1 tsp. dried oregano

1 tsp. thyme

1 large tomato, chopped

Sea salt to taste

Heat frying pan until hot. **Add** safflower oil. When oil is hot, add the veal. **Break it** into small pieces, browning it. **Add** the oregano and thyme as the meat browns. When the meat is browned, add the chopped tomato. **Cook down** until the tomato forms a sauce for the meat. **Add** sea salt to taste, about 1 teaspoonful. Set aside for filling

Mild Taco Sauce

2 T. expeller pressed safflower oil

1 c. chopped leeks

2 large cloves garlic, chopped (about 1 heaping tsp.)

1 c. loosely packed chopped parsley

2 c. chopped red bell pepper

2/3 c. chopped mild green chili pepper (such as banana pepper or cubanel pepper)

1 heaping T. dried oregano

5 c. chopped tomato

1-1/2 tsp. sea salt

Heat oil in a frying pan. When oil is hot, **add** the chopped leeks. **Saute** until the leeks start getting soft. **Add** the garlic. **Saute**. When the garlic is browned, add the parsley, bell pepper, chili pepper and oregano. **Saute** until the peppers are soft. Add the tomatoes and salt. **Cook down** until the tomatoes form a sauce. **Puree** the sauce.

Pizza

No cooking repertoire is complete without pizza! On a yeast free, wheat free, dairy free diet, pizza is a challenge. But if you are willing to expand your vision of what pizza is or should be, you will totally enjoy this one. These are the basic recipes for a rice pizza crust and two pizza sauces. Top with vegetables, or an acceptable rice or soy based cheese.

Rice Pizza Crust

3 c. rice flour (mix brown and white)

3 T. potato starch

3 tsp. baking powder that uses potato starch as a base

1-1/2 tsp. sea salt

1 c. expeller pressed safflower oil

up to 2 c. water

Preheat the oven to 425F. **Mix** the flour with the potato starch, baking powder and salt. **Add** the oil, **mixing** well. This will be a pasty mixture. **Add** water a little at a time until the dough begins to form a ball and pulls away from the sides of the bowl. **Knead** the dough a few times, then spread by pressing out gently over a heated pizza stone or a greased cookie sheet. **Poke holes** in the crust with a fork. **Prebake** the crust for 20 minutes. Now **put the pizza together** (see directions below).

Pizza Sauce

3 T. expeller pressed safflower oil

1/2 c. chopped leek or scallion

1 T. minced fresh garlic

5-1/2 to 6 c. coarsely chopped plum tomatoes

1 T. sea salt

1 T. dried basil

1 T. dried oregano

Heat the oil in a frying pan. Add the leek or scallion and garlic. **Saute** until well browned. **Add** the tomatoes, sea salt and herbs. **Cook** down until the tomatoes form a sauce. Taste for salt. Add more if necessary. This should be fairly salty. **Puree** in a blender or with a hand blender until totally smooth.

Putting the pizza together

Remove the pizza crust from the oven, but **leave the oven on**. **Spread** most of the sauce over the crust. **Reserve** a little for part of the topping. **Top with your favorite foods**. Toppings can be anything you like. We generally chop fresh tomatoes, some leeks or scallions, fresh garlic, vegetables that are handy (even broccoli tastes great on a pizza). Sprinkle these liberally over the pizza sauce. If desired, **sprinkle** some more basil, oregano and salt over the toppings. **Spread** the remaining sauce over the toppings. If you tolerate any type of cheese (soy, rice), grate a liberal amount and **spread it over** the vegetables. The vegetables bake better this way. Put the pizza back in the oven and **bake** at 425F for 20-25 minutes. Remove and eat!

Falafel

Yeast Free • Wheat/Gluten Free
Milk/Casein Free • Egg Free • Cholesterol Free
STAGE IV

Falafel is a popular middle eastern dish. Consisting of seasoned chopped garbanzo beans that are fried into balls, falafel usually is served in pita bread sandwiches accompanied by a sesame sauce called **Tahini Sauce**, lettuce and tomatoes. Makes 50-60 falafels.

3 c. cooked garbanzo beans

2 T. freshly squeezed lemon juice

4 T. water

1 T. minced garlic

2 tsp. sea salt

1/4 tsp. black pepper

2 tsp. dried oregano

1 tsp. dried ground thyme

1/2 tsp. dried ground sage

1/2 tsp. dried tarragon

1 T. expeller pressed safflower oil

1 c. cooked brown rice

3/4 c. rice flour-in mixture

additional rice flour for rolling

expeller pressed safflower oil for frying

Put about half the garbanzos in a **food processor**. Process. **Add** the lemon juice and water and process. **Add** the rest of the garbanzos. Continue to process. **Add** the garlic, salt and herbs. Continue to **process**. The mixture should be somewhat dry and chunky. Add the tablespoon of oil and brown rice. **Process** until fairly smooth. **Remove** from the food processor into a bowl. **Mix in** the rice flour by hand. Allow the mixture to sit for 30 minutes before cooking. **Heat** safflower oil in a frying pan. Pour in enough oil to be about 1/8 inch deep. Put some rice flour on a plate. **Dip out** a teaspoonful of falafel mixture and **drop** it onto the rice flour. **Roll** the falafel around until it is a ball coated with rice flour. When the oil is hot, **place** the falafel balls into the oil. Be careful about splattering oil. **Flatten** slightly. **Cook** until brown and crispy on one side. **Turn over**; **cook** the other side until brown and crispy. **Serve** with chopped lettuce and tomatoes. Deeelicious!

Eggplant Pizza-ettes

Yeast Free • Wheat/Gluten Free
Milk/Casein Free • Egg Free • Cholesterol Free
STAGE IV

When that pizza craving strikes, and you want something quick, this hits the spot. Our daughter, who categorically refuses to eat eggplant, says, "This is superb!"

1 large or 2 small purple eggplants
expeller pressed safflower oil
2-3 tomatoes, sliced into rounds 1/4 inch thick
sea salt
dried basil
dried oregano
dairy free cheese (optional)

Peel the eggplant. **Slice** crosswise into half inch thick rounds. Arrange on a non-stick baking sheet. **Brush** onto each slice a small amount of oil. **Broil** for about 5 minutes, until toasted brown. **Remove** from broiler. Turn over. **Brush** the uncooked side with oil. Broil until browned, about 5 minutes. **Remove** from broiler. **Top** each piece of eggplant with a slice of tomato. Sprinkle with a small amount of salt, basil and oregano. Top with dairy free cheese, if desired. **Broil** for a few minutes until the tomato is browned or the cheese is melted and bubbly.

Fat-Free Stir-Fried Beans

Yeast Free • Wheat/Gluten Free
Milk/Casein Free • Egg Free • Cholesterol Free
STAGE IV

If you're looking for flavor, but don't care for plain beans and if you are trying to avoid adding oil to your beans, these hit the spot. You can use any type of beans. This uses a water stir-frying technique. This recipe feeds 1-2 people.

1/3 c. water
1/3 c. chopped scallions
1/2 tsp. sea salt
1/2 c. chopped tomatoes
1 c. cooked beans

In a non-stick skillet with a cover, bring the water to a **boil**. When boiling, **add** the scallions and sea salt. **Cover**. When the scallions are soft and cooked, **add** the tomatoes. **Stir**. **Cover**. **Cook** until the tomatoes form a sauce. **Stir** and **mash** them down. **Add** the beans. Stir. **Cook** through. Test for salt; add more if necessary. Serve hot.

Potato Blintzes

Yeast Free • Wheat/Gluten Free
Milk/Casein Free (without butter)• Egg Free
• Cholesterol Free (without butter)
STAGE IV

Blintzes are a traditional Jewish dish that consist of crepes filled with some type of filling. This is one of our favorite fillings. Blintzes are always welcome at the table!

2 recipes **Rice Crepes** (page 144)

8 medium red potatoes

water for boiling the potatoes

3 T. butter **or** expeller pressed safflower oil

1 tsp. sea salt

fresh herbs if desired--dill, scallions, chives

hot water from cooked potatoes

expeller pressed safflower oil to grease a pyrex pan

Peel the potatoes. **Cut** them into a few pieces so they cook faster. Put them in a pot and **cover** them with water. Boil. When fork-tender, **drain** them, **reserving** the water. With a fork or potato masher (not an electric mixer), **mash** the potatoes with the butter or oil. **Add** the sea salt and, if desired, about half a handful of chopped fresh herbs. **Mix** with a fork. **Add** hot water to get a desired consistency. The potatoes should be lumpy. **Lightly grease** 9x13 pyrex baking pan. Set aside. Put about 2 T. in the middle of a crepe. **Fold** one side over the potato filling, then the top and bottom, then the other side. **Place** seam side down in the pyrex pan. **Repeat** with the remaining crepes. **Nestle** the blintzes side by side. If desired, dot the blintzes with butter. Cover. Bake at 350F for 45 minutes. Serve hot.

Refried Beans with a Hint of Oregano

Yeast Free • Wheat/Gluten Free
Milk/Casein Free • Egg Free • Cholesterol Free
STAGE IV

2-1/2 c. dried pintos, cooked
3 T. expeller pressed safflower oil
5 scallions, chopped
2 large cloves garlic, chopped
1 white bulb onion, chopped
1 large or 2 small tomatoes, chopped
1 tsp. dried oregano
1/3 tsp. black pepper
1 tsp. sea salt

Drain and rinse the beans. **Heat** the oil in a wok or large frying pan. When the oil is hot, **add** the scallions and onions. **Saute or stir-fry. Add** the garlic. Continue to **stir-fry**. When the onion is slightly browned, **add** the tomatoes. **Cook down** a little. Tomatoes should still hold their shape. **Add** the beans. **Stir** around. **Add** the salt, oregano and pepper. **Cook** through until the beans begin to break apart. **Taste** for salt. Add more if necessary.

South of the Border Pinto Beans

Yeast Free • Wheat/Gluten Free
Milk/Casein Free • Egg Free • Cholesterol Free
STAGE IV

3 T. expeller pressed safflower oil

1/2 cubanel pepper, chopped

2 c. dry pinto beans, cooked

3 scallions, chopped

2 cloves garlic, chopped

1 large tomato, chopped

1 tsp. sea salt, or salt to taste

Heat the oil in a wok. When the oil is hot, **add** the pepper, scallions and garlic. **Saute** until the peppers are browned. **Add** the tomatoes and cook another minute. **Drain and rinse** the beans. Add the beans to the tomato mixture. Add salt. Continue to **cook**. Cook until the beans break apart and have a soft consistency. Taste for salt and add more, if necessary.

Vegetarian Red Rice Chili

Yeast Free • Wheat/Gluten Free
Milk/Casein Free • Egg Free • Cholesterol Free
STAGE IV

This vegetarian chili uses the nutty flavor of red rice in contrast to piquant flavors of scallions and parsley and the sweetness of basil and peppers to give you a taste you will want again and again. Serve with your choice of beans and a green salad for a full meal.

2 T. expeller pressed safflower oil

1 c. chopped red bell pepper

1 c. chopped scallions

1/4 c. packed chopped parsley

1 c. Himalayan or Weihani red rice

1 c. long grain brown rice

2 tsp. sea salt

2 tsp. dried basil

6 c. water

Heat the oil in a 3 quart pot. When hot, **add** the bell pepper and scallions. **Saute** until the pepper is soft. **Add** the parsley and rice. Continue to **saute** for a few minutes. **Add** the salt, basil and water. **Cover**. Bring to a **boil**. Reduce to **simmer**. **Cook** for 50-60 minutes, until the rice is soft. If too much water steams off during cooking, add a little more water, bring to a boil, and simmer until the rice is soft.

Stir-Fried Broccoli and Garbanzo Beans

Yeast Free • Wheat/Gluten Free
Milk/Casein Free • Egg Free • Cholesterol Free
STAGE IV

3 T. expeller pressed safllower oil

4 cloves garlic, minced

4 stalks broccoli, chopped into large pieces (including stems and florets)

Water if necessary

1 tsp. sea salt, or salt to taste

4 c. cooked garbanzo beams

2 T. freshly squeezed lemon juice

1 c. water

2 tsp. potato starch

1 T. water

Heat the oil in a wok. When hot, **add** the garlic. Brown. Add the broccoli. **Stir-fry** until the broccoli is bright and cooked through. **Add** some water, if necessary, to steam the broccoli. Add sea salt to taste. Add the garbanzo beans and lemon juice. **Cook** until hot. **Shove** all of the ingredients up the sides of the wok. **Add** 1 c. water; let the water **boil**. While wating for the water to boil, **mix** 2 tsp. of potato starch in a separate bowl into 1 T. of water. **Gradually mix** the potato starch mixture into the boiling water in the wok. This will thicken the water into a sauce. When thickened, bring the garbanzo beans and broccoli down into the wok. Mix through. Serve immediately.

Garbanzo Beans with Fresh Peppers

Yeast Free • Wheat/Gluten Free
Milk/Casein Free • Egg Free • Cholesterol Free
STAGE IV

This quick and easy bean stir-fry is fresh, beautiful and tasty.

2 T. expeller pressed safflower oil
2 c. dry garbanzo beans, cooked
1 red bell pepper, chopped
1 green bell pepper, chopped
2 scallions, chopped
sea salt to taste

Heat the oil in a wok. When oil is hot, **add** the peppers and scallions. Stir-fry until the peppers are soft. **Add** the beans and salt to taste. **Stir-fry** a few minutes longer. Serve hot.

Stir-Fried Garbanzos with Chinese Long Beans and Asparagus

Yeast Free • Wheat/Gluten Free
Milk/Casein Free • Egg Free • Cholesterol Free
STAGE IV

Chinese long beans are a type of green bean that is about a foot and a half long. They have a wonderfully fresh, but starchy, consistency. If you can find some (usually at an Asian grocery store, good produce store of farmer's market), try this recipe.

> 2 T. expeller pressed safflower oil
>
> 2 cloves garlic, chopped
>
> 1 tsp. minced fresh ginger
>
> 1 lb. Chinese long beans, cut into 1-1/2 to 2 inch lengths
>
> 1 lb. fresh asparagus, cut into 1 inch lengths
>
> 1 tsp. sea salt
>
> 3 c. cooked garbanzo beans
>
> 2 squeezes fresh lemon juice

Heat the oil in a wok. When the oil is hot, **add** the garlic and ginger. **Stir-fry** until the garlic is brown, not burned. **Add** the Chinese long beans. **Stir fry** until the beans are bright. Add the asparagus and salt, continuing to stir-fry. Stir-fry until the vegetables are cooked, a few minutes. Add the cooked garbanzos; mix through and heat. **Taste** for salt. Add more salt if necessary. **Add** the lemon juice and mix through. Cook until hot. Serve hot.

Gourmet Garbanzos

Yeast Free • Wheat/Gluten Free
Milk/Casein Free • Egg Free • Cholesterol Free
STAGE IV

As simple as this dish sounds, it is delicious and goes well with many different types of foods.

Cooked garbanzo beans

Expeller pressed safflower oil

Sea salt

Optional: chopped tomatoes, scallions, red onions for garnish

Measure out the amount of garbanzo beans you would like to use. **Add** about 1 tsp. of oil per cup of beans. **Mix** well. **Sprinkle** on sea salt to taste. Mix. If desired, **mix** in some chopped tomatoes, scallions, and/or red onions for additional flavor and color.

Notes

Pasta and Pasta Sauces

Pasta can be a main dish, a side dish, or just its own dish. . .so we thought pasta deserved its own chapter. You will find the sauces in this chapter fresh and light, easy to make and even easy to freeze to use later. All of the sauces taste great over any kind of pasta-- wheat or rice, or even corn or quinoa; noodles, spaghetti, linguine, fettucine, or any of the countless shapes and sizes in which you can find pasta.

Chunky Pasta Sauce

Yeast Free • Wheat/Gluten Free
Milk/Casein Free • Egg Free • Cholesterol Free
STAGE IV

Rich and hearty, this vegetarian pasta sauce will fill you up on a cold winter night.

2 T. expeller pressed safflower oil

1 T. minced garlic

1 heaping cup chopped leeks

1 heaping cup chopped red bell pepper

10 roma (plum) tomatoes, chopped

2 tsp. dried basil

2 tsp. dried oregano

1 T. sea salt

1/2 tsp. dried thyme

1 tsp. dried dill

1 tsp. dried marjoram

2 c. cooked kidney or pinto beans

1/4-1/2 c. water, if needed

Heat the oil in a large skillet. When hot, add the minced garlic. **Saute.** Be careful not to let the garlic burn. If it starts to burn, lift the pan off the heat and turn down the burner. As the garlic is cooking, **add** the leeks. Saute until the leeks start to get soft. Add the bell pepper. **Saute** until the bell pepper is soft. Add the tomatoes, herbs and salt. Mix well. Cook for a few minutes, then add the cooked beans. Stir. **Cook** over low heat for at least 1 hour, stirring occasionally. If too much liquid evaporates, add some water. The longer the sauce cooks, the better it tastes.

Quick and Easy Pesto

Yeast Free • Wheat/Gluten Free
Milk/Casein Free • Egg Free • Cholesterol Free
STAGE IV

Pesto, a paste of fresh basil, is a real treat during the summer. We buy bunches of basil from the farmer's market, make pesto, and freeze it in ice cube trays. Then, when we want pesto, we just defrost a cube or two and serve on pasta.

> 1-1/2 c. packed fresh basil leaves
> 1-1/2 tsp. sea salt
> 1/2 clove elephant garlic
> 2/3 c. expeller pressed safflower oil

Put the basil leaves and sea salt in a food processor. **Begin processing**. While this is processing, put the elephant garlic in a small bowl and **microwave** on high for 30 seconds, until the garlic gives off liquid. **Add** the garlic and liquid to the basil mixture and continue processing. Slowly add the safflower oil, continuing to **process** the pesto. The pesto is done when the oil is all incorporated. A little pesto goes a long way. **Serve** with pasta, over rice, with vegetables, or with fish, using only a spoonful or two per serving.

Sweet Rosemary Sauce

Yeast Free • Wheat/Gluten Free
Milk/Casein Free (without butter) • Egg Free • Cholesterol
Free (without butter)
STAGE IV

This pasta sauce always gets rave reviews from guests, even children.

2 T. butter or expeller pressed safflower oil

3 c. chopped spring (bulb) onions

3-4 zucchini, sliced in 1/8 inch thick rounds

2 tsp. sea salt

15 plum tomatoes (about 3 lbs.), chopped

1 tsp. dried rosemary, crushed

 or 1 T. fresh rosemary leaves, chopped

2 tsp. dried basil

 or 2 T. fresh basil leaves, finely chopped

2 T. natural honey

Heat the butter or oil in a large frying pan. **Saute** the onions until soft. **Add** the zucchini; saute until soft. Add the salt, tomatoes, and herbs. **Simmer** until the tomatos form a sauce. When the sauce looks about the right consistency, **add** the honey. Serve.

Fresh Basil and Garlic Sauce

Yeast Free • Wheat/Gluten Free
Milk/Casein Free • Egg Free • Cholesterol Free
STAGE IV

This sauce says Wow! with very little effort. This goes very well with **Wilted Spinach Salad** (page 68).

2 T. expeller pressed safflower oil
4 cloves garlic, chopped
1/2 c. packed chopped fresh basil leaves
8 large plum tomatoes, chopped
  or 12 medium plum tomatoes, chopped
1 tsp. sea salt

Heat the oil in a frying pan. **Add** the garlic. **Saute** until the garlic is browned. Add the basil and sea salt. Saute until the basil is wilted. Add the tomatoes and salt. Stir through. Cover and **simmer** until the tomatoes form a sauce. Check the salt and add more if necessary. If you like chunky sauces, serve as is. If you like smooth sauces, **puree** in a blender. Serve over pasta.

Fresh Basil and Oregano Sauce

Yeast Free • Wheat/Gluten Free
Milk/Casein Free • Egg Free • Cholesterol Free
STAGE IV

We have the good fortune to have a yard full of fresh oregano. This began with one tiny plant that grew into a bush, then spread its seeds all over the lawn. Besides smelling great when we mow the lawn, we have an ample supply of fresh oregano.

> 2 T. expeller pressed safflower oil
> 1/2 c. packed chopped fresh basil leaves
> 1/2 c. packed chopped fresh oregano leaves
> 8 large plum tomatoes, chopped
>   **or** 12 medium plum tomatoes, chopped
> 1 tsp. sea salt

Heat the oil in a frying pan. **Add** the basil and oregano leaves. **Saute** until leaves are wilted. Add the tomatoes and salt. Stir through. Cover and **simmer** until the tomatoes form a sauce. Check the salt and add more if necessary. If you like chunky sauces, serve as is. If you like smooth sauces, **puree** in a blender. However, the sauce will be slightly brown due to the green herbs mixing with the red tomatoes. This does not affect taste! Serve over pasta.

Fresh Herb, Leek and Butter Sauce

Yeast Free • Wheat/Gluten Free
Milk/Casein Free (with butter) • Egg Free
STAGE IV

This sauce is out of this world. Try it on rice pasta.

> 3/4 stick of butter
>
> 2 leeks, sliced in rounds
>
> 1/2 c. packed fresh herbs, such as basil, oregano, rosemary, tarragon and chives
>
> 1 tsp. sea salt
>
> 2 boxes, or 20 oz. of rice pasta, cooked according to package directions

Melt the butter in a saucepan. Add the leeks and herbs. Saute. Add the sea salt. Mix. Let rest for 30 minutes or so. Mix through 20 oz. of cooked rice pasta. Serve hot.

Delectable Tomato Ginger Sauce

Yeast Free • Wheat/Gluten Free
Milk/Casein Free • Egg Free • Cholesterol Free
STAGE IV

For an Asian flair, serve beans, rice or pasta--or all three--
with this sauce.

    4 T. expeller pressed safflower oil
    6 scallions, chopped
    4 tsp. minced garlic
    1 tsp. minced fresh ginger
    14 plum tomatoes, chopped
    2 tsp. sea salt
    1 T. white rice flour
    1 T. water

Heat the oil in a wok. **Add** the scallions. **Stir-fry** until bright.
Add the garlic and ginger. Stir-fry. **Add** the tomatoes and
sea salt. **Stir-fry** until the tomatoes are saucy. **Mix** the rice
flour with the extra water. Make sure the sauce is boiling.
Gently **stir** in the rice flour and water mixture. **Cook** until the
sauce is thickened. Serve over beans or pasta.

Sweet Pepper, Tomato, Rosemary and Basil Sauce

Yeast Free • Wheat/Gluten Free
Milk/Casein Free • Egg Free • Cholesterol Free
STAGE IV

This sauce is just what it says--a sweet sauce with delicious vegetables and herbs. Serve over pasta.

> 2 T. expeller pressed safflower oil
>
> 1-1/2 c. chopped sweet red pepper
>
> 18 plum tomatoes, chopped
>
> 2 tsp. dried basil
>
> 1-1/2 tsp. dried rosemary, crushed
>
> 2 tsp. sea salt

Heat the oil in a frying pan. **Add** the red peppers. **Saute** until the peppers start to get soft. **Add** the tomatoes, herbs and salt. **Cook** until the tomatoes form a sauce. Serve over pasta "as is" (chunky), or puree for a smooth sauce.

Anniversary Sauce

Yeast Free • Wheat/Gluten Free
Milk/Casein Free (without butter) • Egg Free • Cholesterol
Free (without butter)
STAGE IV

Using any excuse to celebrate, we created this sauce in honor of the anniversary of our home ownership. It's great any time!

> 2 T. expeller pressed safflower oil
>
> 1-1/2 c. chopped red bell peppers
>
> 1 c. chopped white bulb onion or leek
>
> 1 c. loosely packed chopped fresh parsley
>
> 5 fist-sized tomatoes, chopped
>
> 2 tsp. sea salt
>
> 2 tsp. natural honey
>
> 2 squeezes of a fresh lemon
>
> 1 T. butter (optional)

Heat the oil in a frying pan. When hot, **add** the pepper, onion and parsley. **Saute**. When the peppers are soft, add the tomatoes. **Cook** until the tomatoes form a sauce. **Mix in** the honey and lemon. If desired, mix in the butter. Serve chunky or **puree** in a blender. Serve over pasta.

Tarragon Basil Sauce

Yeast Free • Wheat/Gluten Free
Milk/Casein Free • Egg Free • Cholesterol Free
STAGE IV

The tarragon and basil in this sauce make it delicately sweet.

2 tsp. expeller pressed safflower oil
1 c. chopped red bell pepper
1 tsp. dried tarragon
1 T. fresh chopped basil leaves
   or 1 tsp. dried basil
6 c. coarsely chopped tomatoes
1 tsp. sea salt

Heat the oil in a frying pan. When the oil is hot, **add** the bell pepper. **Saute** until the pepper is soft. **Add** the herbs, tomatoes and salt. **Stir**. **Cook** until the tomatoes form a sauce. **Puree** in a blender. Serve hot over pasta.

Succulent Bell Pepper Sauce

Yeast Free • Wheat/Gluten Free
Milk/Casein Free • Egg Free • Cholesterol Free
STAGE IV

Adding rosemary and sage to basil and tarragon creates a completely different flavor that is irresistible at the table.

2 T. expeller pressed safflower oil

10-12 plum tomatoes, chopped

2 c. coarsely chopped sweet red bell pepper

2 tsp. sea salt

1 tsp. dried basil

large pinch dried tarragon

1/8 tsp. dried sage powder

1 tsp. dried rosemary leaves, crushed

water, if needed

Heat the oil in a frying pan. When hot, **add** the tomatoes and peppers. **Saute** until the tomatoes start to break apart. **Add** the salt and herbs. **Saute** until the tomatoes form a sauce, usually about 20 minutes. **Puree** in a blender. Add some water if the sauce is too thick. Serve hot over rice pasta.

Columbus Spaghetti Sauce

Yeast Free • Wheat/Gluten Free
Milk/Casein Free • Egg Free • Cholesterol Free
STAGE IV

We created this sauce while on an extended visit to Columbus, Ohio--hence the name. But you can eat it anywhere!

2 T. expeller pressed safflower oil

1 red onion, chopped

2 cloves garlic, chopped

1 bunch fresh parsley, chopped

1 tsp. dried basil

1 tsp. dried rosemary leaves, crushed

1 tsp. dried thyme

5-6 plum tomatoes, chopped

1 tsp. sea salt

Heat the oil in a frying pan. When hot, **add** the onion and garlic. **Saute** until both are browned. **Add** the parsley. **Saute** a minute longer. **Add** the herbs, tomatoes and salt. **Cook** until the tomatoes are soft and form a sauce. Taste for salt. Add more if necessary.

Grandma Jeanine's Texas Hash, Veggie Style

Yeast Free • Wheat/Gluten Free
Milk/Casein Free • Egg Free • Cholesterol Free
STAGE IV

One of our all-time favorite pasta dishes is this Texas Hash from Grandma Jeanine Semon. It doesn't really have hash, and really isn't from Texas, but it's great! What makes this recipe luscious is that the noodles are cooked in the moisture and flavor of the opnions and pepper instead of in water.

6T. (divided) expeller pressed safflower oil

4 medium sized fresh onions, chopped chunky

1 medium green bell pepper, chopped chunky

2 large cloves garlic, chopped chunky

5 medium to large tomatoes, cut in large chunks

1 pkg. (8-10 oz.) rice noodles (seashell,spiral or penne)

2 tsp. sea salt

1/4 tsp. black pepper

up to 1-1/2 c. water, divided

Heat 3 T. of oil in a skillet. When hot, **add** the onions, pepper and garlic. **Saute** until the onions glisten. **Add** the tomatoes and the noodles. **Sprinkle** the salt, pepper, an additional 2 T. oil and 3/4 c. water, and mix together lightly. Place in a 3 quart casserole, cover, and **bake** at 350F for 40 minutes, remove the cover, add 1/4 to 1/2 c. water plus one T. safflower oil and mix the ingredients lightly to moisten the surface noodles. **Cover and place back** in the oven for another 20 minutes. Be careful not to overcook the noodles! Serve hot.

Notes

Side Dishes

Vegetables, rice, potatoes, yams, and even flatbreads and crepes round out every meal. You will find delicious choices here to satisfy your palate!

 Flatbreads and Crepes

 Rice

 Potatoes and Yams

 Vegetables

Rice Flatbread

Yeast Free • Wheat/Gluten Free
Milk/Casein Free • Egg Free • Cholesterol Free
STAGE IV

This rice flatbread, modeled on tortillas, is the closest we have come to devising something that has the feeling of bread. All of our children love it. The main problem we encounter is being unable to get enough from the pan to the dinner table because it gets eaten in between!

1/2 c. brown rice flour

1/2 c. white rice flour

1 tsp. sea salt

3 T. expeller pressed safflower oil

1/2 to 3/4 c. water

Mix the brown and white rice flours together with the sea salt. **Add** the oil. Mix well until pea-sized balls form in the flour. Gradually add the water, mixing well, until the water is blended in. The rice should stick together like dough. If it does not, add a little more water. **Heat** a non-stick skillet on medium-high heat. **Form** thin patties with your hands. As you form each patty, **place** it on the hot frying pan. **Grill** until the patty starts to get brown spots. Do not burn! **Turn over** and grill the other side. **Remove** when the second side has brown spots. These are delicious plain, topped with honey, spread with butter, or as a base for pizza or tacos.

Rice Crepes

Yeast Free • Wheat/Gluten Free
Milk/Casein Free • Egg Free • Cholesterol Free
STAGE IV

These crepes are versatile and have a nice flavor, but do not overpower other ingredients. You can use them for wrappers around sweet or savory fillings. They are especially good for blintzes, or even as a soft tortilla for tacos. This recipe makes 7-9 crepes.

> 1/2 c. white rice flour
>
> 1/2 c. brown rice flour
>
> 4 T. potato starch
>
> 1/2 tsp. sea salt
>
> 2 T. expeller pressed safflower oil
>
> 1-1/2 c. water
>
> expeller pressed safflower oil to grease pan

Use a 9-inch crepe pan. With a wire whisk, **mix** the dry ingredients together (flours, starch and sea salt). **Whisk** in the oil, then the water. Make sure the batter is not lumpy. **Heat** the pan until it is hot enough that a drop of water rolls around, but does not boil. Put a few drops of oil in the pan. Carefully **spread the oil** around with a wadded-up paper towel. **Pour** a small amount of batter in the pan, **tilting** the pan around until the batter covers the bottom of the pan in a thin layer. **Cook** until air pockets start to bubble. Using a lightly greased spatula, **turn** the crepe over. **Lightly brown** on the other side. When done, **flip** out onto a plate. Lightly grease the pan again and **repeat**.

Potato Crepes or Passover Noodles

Yeast Free • Wheat/Gluten Free
Milk/Casein Free
STAGE IV

These crepes can be made salty or sweet, and can be eaten alone, with butter and salt, with fruit inside, or with vegetables--in short, any way you want. These are a great wrapper for blintzes as well. Makes 8-9 crepes. We call these Passover Noodles because on the holiday of Passover, you can slice these up and eat them like noodles. However, usually we don't have enough to slice up!

> 2 eggs
> 1/2 c. acceptable rice milk **or** water
> 4 T. potato starch
> 1/2 tsp. sea salt
> 1 T. expeller pressed safflower oil
> Optional: 1/2 tsp. any herbs or spices
> expeller pressed safflower oil for cooking

Blend all ingredients except the oil for cooking in blender. **Heat** a 9-inch skillet over medium heat until a drop of water rolls around the surface. **Wipe** the skillet with oil. **Pour** a small amount of batter in the skillet. **Swirl** it to cover the surface of the skillet. **Cook** until golden brown and the crepe turns easily. **Flip**. **Cook** on the other side until golden. Flip out of the pan and repeat until the batter is gone. You may need to re-oil the pan between crepes. You may also need to turn on the blender between crepes.

Rice with Lemon Grass

Yeast Free • Wheat/Gluten Free
Milk/Casein Free • Egg Free • Cholesterol Free
STAGE IV

This easy rice has the subtle taste of lemon, reminiscent of Thai and Vietnamese rice. We use lemon grass instead of fresh lemon. Lemon grass is available in Asian markets and sometimes in good produce stores. Try this for something different!

    3 stalks lemon grass
    2 c. raw long grain brown rice
    1 tsp. sea salt
    4-1/2 to 5 c. water

Prepare the lemon grass by peeling off the tough outer layers. **Slice vertically** down the middle, then cut into three inch lengths. Put the rice in a pot or rice **steamer**. **Mix** the lemon grass and salt with the rice. **Put** the water in the rice. If using a pot, put in 4-1/2 c. water. **Cover**. Bring to a **boil,** then stir once. Reduce to **simmer**. Cook for 50 minutes, or until rice is soft and cooked. If using a steamer, cook the rice according to your usual method.

Baked Rice with Sweet Peppers and Basil

Yeast Free • Wheat/Gluten Free
Milk/Casein Free • Egg Free • Cholesterol Free
STAGE IV

This casserole is an easy alternative to stuffed peppers. It has all the flavor of the peppers, and the looks, without the time consuming and sometimes difficult task of stuffing them. This dish is a welcome change to ordinary steamed rice. It comes out light and fluffy, and with the basil and red pepper, looks as good as it tastes.

2 T. expeller pressed safllower oil

2 c. chopped leek

2 large cloves garlic, chopped

1/2 c. packed chopped fresh basil leaves

2 c. chopped zucchini or summer squash

2-1/2 c. long grain brown rice

6 c. water

1-1/2 T. sea salt

4 red bell peppers, cut in half

Preheat the oven to 375F. **Heat** the oil in a frying pan. When hot, **add** the leeks and garlic. **Saute** until the leek is soft. Then add the basil and saute. **Add** the zucchini. Saute until soft. Add the rice. **Saute** until the rice is browned. **Pour** the rice mixture into a deep 9x13 pyrex pan. **Add** the water and sea salt. **Lay** the halves of the bell peppers over the rice, hollow side down. **Bake** at 375 F. for 1-1/2 to 2 hours, until the rice is fluffy.

Toasted Rice & Veggies

Yeast Free • Wheat/Gluten Free
Milk/Casein Free • Egg Free • Cholesterol Free
STAGE IV

4 T. expeller pressed safflower oil, divided

1 T. chopped Cubanel pepper, or other mild chili pepper

4 c. chopped broccoli

1 c. chopped green beans

2 c. chopped zucchini

2 c. chopped broccoli

2 tsp. sea salt, divided

1 tsp. dried basil

1 tsp. dried rosemary, crushed

2 c. raw brown rice

1 c. chopped tomatoes

5 c. boiling water

Heat 2 T. safflower oil in a large skillet the has a cover. When hot, **add** the chili pepper, broccoli, green beans, zucchini, broccoli and 1 tsp. sea salt. **Saute** until the vegetables are soft. **Add** the basil and rosemary and saute another minute or two. **Remove** the vegetables and put on a plate or in a bowl. **Heat** the other 2 T. safflower oil in the frying pan. When hot, add the brown rice. Stirring frequently, **toast** the rice in the oil until most of the rice has browned. **Add** the additional sea salt and tomatotes. **Mix** through. Add the boiling water. Cover, bring to a **boil** (if necessary), reduce to a **simmer.** Cook 50-60 minutes, until the rice is fluffy.

Chickenless Chicken and Rice

Yeast Free • Wheat/Gluten Free
Milk/Casein Free (without butter) • Egg Free
• Cholesterol Free (without butter)
STAGE IV

One of our very favorite casseroles, inspired by Jeanine Semon, this dish tastes like it has chicken in it--but of course, it doesn't. We never have leftovers.

1-1/2 c. long grain brown rice

4 carrots, chopped in large pieces

1 leek, chopped

3 c. red potatoes, peeled and cubed

1-1/2 tsp. sea salt

1 T. butter

    or 1 T. expeller pressed safflower oil

4 c. boiling water

Preheat the oven to 375F. Put all ingredients into a 1-1/2 quart covered casserole dish. **Mix** well. **Cover**. **Bake** at 375F for 60 minutes.

Veggie Potato Bake

Yeast Free • Wheat/Gluten Free
Milk/Casein Free • Egg Free • Cholesterol Free
STAGE IV

This casserole is the potato equivalent of **Chickenless Chicken and Rice.** Kids love it.

> 3 c. red potatoes, cubed and peeled
> 2 c. chopped cauliflower
> 2 c. chopped broccoli
> 1-2 tsp. sea salt (to taste)
> 1/2 c. water

Preheat the oven to 375F. **Put** the potatoes, cauliflower and broccoli in a 1-1/2 quart covered casserole dish. **Sprinkle** with sea salt, to taste. Put the water in the casserole. **Mix. Cover. Bake** at 375F for one hour, or until the potatoes are soft.

Very Sweet Potato Kugel

Yeast Free • Wheat/Gluten Free
Milk/Casein Free • Egg Free • Cholesterol Free
STAGE IV

A kugel is a baked pudding, traditionally made with eggs and a variety of other delicious ingredients. Kugels usually are either sweet or salty. This potato kugel is both sweet and salty--the sweetness comes from the yams and honey. Instead of using eggs, we use the natural starch from the potatoes to hold it together. Try it for something different.

> 3 very large (12 oz.) russet potatoes
>> or 6 medium russet potatoes
>
> 1 large yam
> 1/3 c. natural honey
> 2 T. expeller pressed safflower oil
> 1-1/2 tsp. sea salt
> 1-1/2 tsp. freshly squeezed lemon juice
> expeller pressed safflower oil for greasing baking dish

Preheat the oven to 375F. **Peel and grate** the russet potatoes and the yam, by hand or in a food processor. **Take out** about 3 cups of the potato mixture and **puree** in a food processor, using the processing blade of a food processor. **Combine** all ingredients in a bowl and mix together. **Pour** into a 7x11 oiled pyrex baking pan. **Cover tightly** with foil. **Bake** at 375F for 90 minutes. **Uncover**. **Broil** for 5-10 minutes until the top browns slightly.

Hash Brown Potatoes and Variations

Yeast Free • Wheat/Gluten Free
Milk/Casein Free • Egg Free • Cholesterol Free
STAGE IV

Hash browns are a staple of our diet. We eat them for breakfast, take them as leftovers for lunch, and even eat them for snacks and dinner! You can make as many varieties of hash browns as you have imagination. Here is the basic recipe, with some variations. There are two tricks to making great hash browns. First, start with a very hot frying pan. If you put potatotes into cold oil, they will turn gray before they cook and will look very unappetizing. Second, do not skimp on salt. Salt can make or break this very simple dish! Start with the amount you think you need, then taste when done. Add more if necessary.

Basic Hash Browns

> 4 russet potatoes, peeled
>
> 2-3 T. expeller pressed safflower oil
>
> 1/2 tsp. sea salt or more, to taste

Put a large, non-stick frying pan on the stove to **heat**. This works best with a frying pan curved at the edges. When the pan is hot, **add** the oil. Meanwhile, **cut** the potatoes in half both lengthwise and crosswise. **Remove** any bad spots. **Grate** the potatoes by hand or with a food processor. By now the oil should be hot enough that a piece of grated potato sizzles in the oil, but does not burn. If not, continue to heat. When the oil is hot, slide the potatoes into the pan. Spread around. Liberally sprinkle with salt. Turn frequently. Fry until the potatoes are crispy and golden brown on the outside, but soft and creamy on the inside. Serve hot.

Variation 1: Hash Browns with Scallions

In addition to the ingredients for Basic Hash Browns, chop up 3 scallions. **After** the oil is hot, but **before** you put the potatoes in, **slide** the scallions into the oil and saute them until they are soft. Then continue with the recipe for Basic Hash Browns.

Variation 2: Hash Browns with Tomatoes

In addition to the ingredients for Basic Hash Browns, chop up one tomato. **After** the oil is hot, but **before** you put the potatoes in, **slide** the tomato pieces into the oil and saute them until they are just slightly soft. Then continue with the recipe for Basic Hash Browns.

Variation 3: Hash Browns with Peppers

In addition to the ingredients for Basic Hash Browns, chop up 1/2 c. red and/or green bell pepper. **After** the oil is hot, but **before** you put the potatoes in, **slide** the peppers into the oil and saute them until they are soft. Then continue with the recipe for Basic Hash Browns.

Variation 4: Hash Browns with Everything!

In addition to the ingredients for Basic Hash Browns, chop up 3 scallions, 1/2 tomato, 1/2 red and/or green bell pepper, and a small piece of red onion. **After** the oil is hot, but **before** you put the potatoes in, **slide** the vegetables into the oil and saute them until they are soft. Then continue with the recipe for Basic Hash Browns.

Cranberry Tzimmes

Yeast Free • Wheat/Gluten Free
Milk/Casein Free • Egg Free • Cholesterol Free
STAGE IV

Tzimmes is a traditional, slow-cooked Jewish side dish. It often is served on Passover. This tzimmes uses an unusual combination of foods to serve up an utterly delightful taste.

2 large yams, peeled and cubed in bite-sized cubes

2 large pears, peeled and cubed

5 T. freshly squeezed lemon juice

1 c. fresh or freshly frozen cranberries

1/2 c. water

Preheat oven to 375F. **Mix** all ingredients in a pyrex casserole dish. Cover. **Bake** at 375F for 90 minutes, stirring every 30 minutes.

Stir-Fried Yams and Ginger

Yeast Free • Wheat/Gluten Free
Milk/Casein Free • Egg Free • Cholesterol Free
STAGE IV

If you are looking for something really different, try this. Not only will its appearance please you, with its orange and green, but its taste will surprise you.

> 4 scallions cut in 1/2 lengthwise then crosswise into 3" strips
>
> 2 tsp. minced ginger
>
> 1 large or 2 small yams peeled and cut into thin half moons between 1/16 and 1/8 inches thick
>
> Safflower oil for stir fry
>
> 1 tsp. sea salt
>
> 1/2 c. water

Heat oil in a wok or frying pan. **Add** scallions and ginger. **Stir fry** until scallions are soft. **Add** yams and salt. **Stir fry** until yams are browned. **Add** water. Put cover on wok. **Steam** until yams are cooked. If desired, add salt to taste.

Baked Potatoes

Yeast Free • Wheat/Gluten Free
Milk/Casein Free • Egg Free • Cholesterol Free
STAGE IV

This recipe is for basic baked potatoes. Our family often enjoys baked potatoes with dinner or even for after school snacks. Try different kinds of potatoes. Russet potatoes are flaky and fluffy. Red potatoes are creamy. Yukon Golds have their own unique flavor.

> Potatoes
>
> Toppings: chopped scallions, butter (if desired), minced chives, fresh dill
>
> Sea salt to taste

Thoroughly scub as many potatoes as you need. **Pierce** each potato a few times with a fork. **For oven baking**, preheat the oven to 350F. Wrap each potato in foil. Pierce the foil. Lay the potatoes directly on the rack. Bake at 350F for 60 to 90 minutes, depending on the side of the potato. The potatoes should squish when you squeeze them. **For microwave baking,** place the potatoes in the microwave (unwrapped and uncovered). If your microwave has an automatic sensor, press "potatoes" and wait! If not, allow about 5 minutes per potato for average sized russet potatoes, less for red potatoes, more for jumbo potatoes. **When you are ready to serve**, while potatoes are still hot, sqeeze the potatoes lightly between your fingers to loosen up the insides. Cut the potatoes down the middle, both lengthwise and width-wise, so you have an "x" on the top. Take a fork and fluff up the potato insides several times, poking the insides around. This makes the potatoes light and fluffy. Put your toppings in or on top, and serve.

Baked Acorn Squash with Honey

Yeast Free • Wheat/Gluten Free
Milk/Casein Free • Egg Free • Cholesterol Free
STAGE IV

What better way to serve acorn squash than baked with honey?

> acorn squash--1/2 squash per person
> natural honey

Preheat the oven to 350F. **Cut** each squash in half, scooping out the seeds. **Slice** a piece of the bottom so each half sits flat in a covered casserole dish. **Place** the squash in the casserole dish. **Drizzle** honey over all of the squash. **Cover**. **Bake** at 350F for 60 minutes, or until fork tender.

Zucchini Fingers

Yeast Free • Wheat/Gluten Free
Milk/Casein Free • Egg Free • Cholesterol Free
STAGE IV

When you are craving something deep-fried, try these
Zucchini Fingers. These are delicious and really hit the spot.
Dip in **Homemade Mayonnaise** (page 83) or **Basil
Mayonnaise** (page 84), **Hot Salsa** (page 86), or **Almost
Barbeque Sauce** from **Feast Without Yeast**.

> 5-6 medium zucchini
> 1 c. rice flour
> 1 tsp. dried basil
> 1 tsp. dried oregano
> 1/2 tsp. sea salt
> expeller pressed safflower oil

Slice the zucchini into "fingers" by slicing lengthwise into 4-6
wedges, then crosswise. You will get 6-8 zucchini fingers per
zucchini. Start **heating** some safflower oil in a frying pan.
An electric frying pan works especially well, because the
temperature stays contant. This recipe also uses a lot of oil,
so have a bottle handy. While the oil is heating, **combine** the
flour, basil, oregano and salt in a lunch-sized paper bag.
Put in a handful of "fingers." **Shake** well to coat. **Remove
and repeat** with the remainder of the zucchini. Meanwhile,
when the oil is hot but not smoky, **carefully place** some
fingers in it. Brown on one side, then gently turn with two
forks to cook the other sides evenly. They are done when
browned and fork-tender. **Remove** the first batch and if
desired, **drain** on brown paper bags or on a rack over a
plate. **Repeat** with subsequent batches of fingers, adding
more oil as necessary. Serve hot.

Steamed Vegetables

Yeast Free • Wheat/Gluten Free
Milk/Casein Free • Egg Free • Cholesterol Free
STAGE IV

This recipe is for basic steamed vegetables, a staple with any meal. For variety, try cutting the vegetables in different ways. Sometimes slice the vegetables. Sometimes make spears. Sometimes cook them whole. Try different combinations of vegetables, too, to see what you like. You can cook most vegetables together. The only exception is brussels sprouts, which take so long to cook that you will over cook everything else.

> chopped fresh vegetables, any type
> water
> sea salt, if desired

Wash the vegetables Put the vegetables in a pot that you fill about two thirds full. Add about half an inch of water to one inch of water. If desired, sprinkle a small amount of sea salt over the vegetables. This helps keep them green, but does add salt to the meal. Cover. Bring to a boil. Reduce the heat so the steam is still vigorous, but you are not boiling the vegetables. Cook until the vegetables are just a shade darker than bright green and fork tender. Remove the top of the pot and remove the vegetables from the heat, or they will over cook. Seve hot.

Rosemary Roasted Vegetables

Yeast Free • Wheat/Gluten Free
Milk/Casein Free • Egg Free • Cholesterol Free
STAGE IV

The flavors of the yams, parsnips, carrots, rosemary and peppers blend together and carmelize for one of the best vegetable dishes we have made. This tastes better if you make it several hours before serving, or even a day ahead, to allow the flavors to develop fully.

> 2 large yams
>
> 5 large parsnips
>
> 5 large carrots
>
> 1 large red bell pepper
>
> 1 tsp. dried rosemary leaves, crushed
>
> 2 tsp. sea salt
>
> 4 T. expeller pressed safflower oil

Preheat the oven to 375F. **Peel** the yams, parsnips and carrots. **Cut** them into pieces 2-3 inches long and no more than 1/2 inch thick and wide. **Slice** the bell pepper into sticks about 1/4 inch wide. **Mix** all vegetables together in a 9x13 pyrex pan. **Sprinkle** the rosemary and salt over the vegetables. **Pour** the oil over the vegetables. **Put** clean (preferably new) plastic or other kitchen gloves on your hands. With your gloved hands, **mix** the oil, rosemary and salt through the vegetables, distributing it thoroughly. **Roast** uncovered at 375F for 90 minutes, removing from the oven and mixing well every 20 minutes. Let stand at least 2 hours before serving.

Vegetable Stuffing

Yeast Free • Wheat/Gluten Free
Milk/Casein Free • Egg Free • Cholesterol Free
STAGE IV

We developed this recipe as an alternative to traditional "high carb" stuffing for some guests who were on a "low carb" diet. The stuffing turned out to be so delicious that we would recommend it any time! This stuffing recipe makes enough to stuff on 15-lb. turkey with vegetables also cooked outside the turkey. Chop all vegetables in large pieces.

2-1/2 c. chopped zucchini

2-1/2 c. chopped red bell pepper

4-5 c. peeled and chopped carrots, in one inch lengths

4 c. chunked bulb onions, leeks, scallions, or combination

4 cloves garlic, peeled and halved

4 medium red potatoes, peeled and cut into eighths

1 tsp.each : celery seed, dried basil, dill seed, dried thyme, and dried sage powder

1 bay leaf

1-1/2 tsp. dried marjoram

3 tsp. sea salt.

Mix all ingredients together in a large bowl. **Stuff** the neck and body cavity of a turkey, sewing the neck flap closed. If you have leftover vegetables, place them on the bottom of a roasting pan or in the turkey roasting bag. **Prepare** the turkey as usual for roasting. Roast according to your usual method for stuffed turkeys. When done, **unstuff** the turkey. Put the stuffing in a bowl with liquid from the turkey. Keep in a warm (200F) oven until serving time.

Braised Parsnips and Carrots

Yeast Free • Wheat/Gluten Free
Milk/Casein Free • Egg Free • Cholesterol Free
STAGE IV

2 T. expeller pressed safflower oil

1 clove elephant garlic, chopped

2 shallots, chopped

5 medium parsnips, peeled and sliced into 3 inch match sticks

2 carrots, peeled and sliced into 3 inch match sticks

1/2 tsp. sea salt

Heat the oil in a wok or frying pan. When hot, **add** the elephant garlic and shallots. **Saute** until the garlic is browned, but not burned. **Add** parsnips and carrots, stirring them around and browning them. Add the sea salt. Continue to **braise** the parsnips and carrots until they are browned. Serve hot.

Roasted Eggplant

Yeast Free • Wheat/Gluten Free
Milk/Casein Free • Egg Free • Cholesterol Free
STAGE IV

2 large eggplants

1-1/2 tsp. sea salt

1 clove elephant garlic

4 T. expeller pressed safflower oil

Preheat the oven to 375F. Have a 9x13 pyrex pan ready.
Peel the eggplants. **Cut** them into 1/2 inch cubes. Put the
cubes in the pyrex pan. They will overfill the pan. Sprinkle
the salt over the eggplant. **Chop** the garlic into small pieces
and sprinkle it over the eggplant. **Pour** the oil over all. With
plastic or vinyl gloves on, **mix** the
oil, salt and garlic through the
eggplant by hand to coat the
eggplant evenly. **Roast**
uncovered for 60 minutes,
removing from the oven every 20
minutes to **stir** the eggplant
around.

Stir-Fried Sugar Snap Peas

Yeast Free • Wheat/Gluten Free
Milk/Casein Free • Egg Free • Cholesterol Free
STAGE IV

Sugar snap peas, in season, need almost no seasoning, and taste divine. Stir-frying takes them to an even higher level.

> 1 pound sugar snap pea pods
> 2 T. expeller pressed safflower oil
> sea salt to taste

Prepare the peas by snapping off one end of the pod and pulling the string off. Wash and drain well. Heat the oil in a wok, until the oil is hot. Add the pea pods. Quickly stir fry for about a minute. Sprinkle over sea salt to taste. Stir fry a few seconds more. Remove from heat. Serve hot!

Dad's Favorite
Tomato and Eggplant Stir-Fry

Yeast Free • Wheat/Gluten Free
Milk/Casein Free • Egg Free • Cholesterol Free
STAGE IV

For flavor, you can't beat this stir-fry! Dad loves it!

3 T. expeller pressed safflower oil

1 c. sliced red bell pepper

1 scallion, sliced

1 clove garlic, chopped (optional)

1 large purple eggplant, peeled and cubed (about 8 cups)

4 medium red tomatoes

1-1/2 to 1-3/4 tsp. sea salt, to taste

Heat the oil in a wok. When the oil is hot, **add** the pepper and scallion. If desired, add the garlic. **Stir-fry** until the onion gets soft. Add the eggplant and tomato. Continue **stir-frying** until the eggplant is soft and the tomatoes form a sauce. Add the salt to taste. Serve hot!

Sweet & Sour Chinese Vegetables

Yeast Free • Wheat/Gluten Free
Milk/Casein Free • Egg Free • Cholesterol Free
STAGE IV

The tangy, sweet taste of these vegetables satisfies every palate. Serve over brown rice.

2-5 T. expeller-pressed safflower oil

3 scallions, chopped

2 tsp. minced fresh garlic

2 tsp. minced fresh ginger

2 c. red pepper, sliced into thin strips

2 c. chopped broccoli

2 c. chopped green beans, in 1-inch lengths

1/2 c. freshly squeezed lemon juice

1/2 c. natural honey

1/4 -1/2 c. water

2-3 T. potato starch

sea salt to taste

Heat 2 T. of safflower oil in the wok. When hot, **add** the scallions, ginger and garlic. **Stir-fry** until the garlic starts to brown, but not burn. **Add** the peppers. **Sprinkle** with salt. **Stir-fry** until the pepper is soft. **Remove** all from the wok. **Repeat**, cooking each vegetable separately, sprinkled with a small amount of sea salt. When the last vegetable is cooked, put the rest of the vegetables, garlic and ginger back in the wok. **Mix. Taste** for salt; add more if desired. Mix the honey and lemon juice together in a bowl. **Pour over** the vegetables and mix through. **Push** the vegetables up the sides of the wok. The liquid will collect at the bottom. While the liquid is heating, **mix** the potato starch in a bowl with 1/4 c. of the water. When the liquid in the wok starts to boil, **stir** in the potato starch/water mixture. Keep stirring. This will thicken into a nice glaze. If the sauce becomes too thick, thin with a little water. Bring the vegetables back down and mix into the sauce. Serve immediately.

Sweet and Sour Purple Cabbage

Yeast Free • Wheat/Gluten Free
Milk/Casein Free • Egg Free • Cholesterol Free
STAGE IV

Add color and a different taste to your meal with this sweet and sour purple cabbage. A favorite of children and adults alike. The best part is in the cooking. When you add the lemon juice, the cabbage turns color!

1 head purple cabbage
2 T. expeller pressed safflower oil
1 tsp. celery seed
1 tsp. sea salt
2 T. freshly squeezed lemon juice
2 T. natural honey

Shred the cabbage. Set aside. **Heat** the oil in a wok. When the oil is hot, **add** the cabbage and celery seed. **Stir-fry**. **Sprinkle** the sea salt over the cabbage while stir-frying. When the cabbage is soft, **mix in** the lemon juice. Watch the cabbage turn colors! **Mix in** the honey. Remove from heat; serve hot.

Quick 'N Easy Ratatouille

Yeast Free • Wheat/Gluten Free
Milk/Casein Free • Egg Free • Cholesterol Free
STAGE IV

Want a delicious alternative to the cutting, slicing and layering of traditional Ratatouille? Try this. It takes about 10 minutes to put together, an hour and a half to bake, and no time at all to eat!

expeller pressed safflower oil

1 medium eggplant

2 c. chopped tomatoes

1 tsp. minced garlic

1 tsp. sea salt

1 tsp. dried basil

1 tsp. dried oregano

Preheat the oven to 375 F. Lightly oil a medium-sized casserole dish. **Peel** the eggplant. Cut it into 1/2 inch cubes. Place in the casserole dish. **Add** the tomatoes, garlic, salt, basil and oregano. Mix well. **Cover. Bake** at 375 F. for about an hour and a half (90 minutes). Remove from the oven. Stir to mix the flavors. The eggplant will be soft and will fall apart. Serve hot!

Steamed Artichokes

Yeast Free • Wheat/Gluten Free
Milk/Casein Free • Egg Free • Cholesterol Free
STAGE IV

Artichokes are delectible under any circumstances. We make them plain, and serve them with **Celery Seed Mayonnaise** (page 84).

> Artichokes-one per person
> Water

Prepare the artichokes by washing them thoroughly, separating the leaves when possible. Take off the tough outer leaves. With scissors, cut off the thorny ends of the leaves. **Cut the stems** down to about 1/4 inch. **Stand** the artichokes in a large pot. **Add** water to about half the depth of the artichokes. Cover. Bring to a **boil.** Reduce to simmer. Cook until the top leaves easily peel off.

Stir-Fried Collard Greens

Yeast Free • Wheat/Gluten Free
Milk/Casein Free • Egg Free • Cholesterol Free
STAGE IV

Our family loves stir-fried collard greens. They are sweet and rich. A bonus is that collard greens are high in calcium and B vitamins. This recipes comes to us from our dear friend, Vannie Lee Henning.

1 large bunch collard greens
pot of boiling water
2 T. expeller pressed safflower oil
1 bunch of scallions or 1 large leek, chopped
2 large tomatoes, chopped
sea salt to taste

Remove spines from the collard greens. Coarsely **chop** the leaves. **Plunge** into boiling water for 30 seconds, then remove with a slotted spoon. **Drain** and set aside. **Heat** oil in wok; add scallions or leeks. **Stir-fry** until browned. Add the tomatoes. Stir-fry until the tomatoes make a sauce. **Add** the collards and stir-fry another minute or so. Add sea salt to taste. Serve hot!

Eggplant Fingers

Yeast Free • Wheat/Gluten Free
Milk/Casein Free • Egg Free • Cholesterol Free
STAGE IV

When you are craving something deep-fried, try these eggplant fingers. Try **Zucchini Fingers** (page 158) if you don't like eggplant.   These are delicious and really hit the spot. Dip in **Homemade Mayonnaise** (page 83) or **Basil Mayonnaise** (page 84), **Hot Salsa** (page86), or **Almost Barbeque Sauce** from **Feast Without Yeast.**.

1 large or 2 small eggplants

1 c. rice flour

1 tsp. dried basil

1 tsp. dried oregano

1/2 tsp. sea salt

expeller pressed safflower oil

Peel the eggplant. **Slice** into "fingers" about 2-3 inches long and 1/2 inch squared. Start **heating** some safflower oil in a frying pan. An electric frying pan works especially well, because the temperature stays contant. This recipe also uses a lot of oil, so have a bottle handy. While the oil is heating, **combine** the flour, basil, oregano and salt in a lunch-sized paper bag. **Put in** a handful of "fingers." **Shake** well to coat. **Remove and repeat** with the remainder of the eggplant. Meanwhile, when the oil is hot but not smoky, **carefully place** some fingers in it. Brown on one side, then gently turn with two forks to cook the other sides evenly. They are done when browned and fork-tender. **Remove** the first batch and if desired, **drain** on brown paper bags or on a rack over a plate. **Repeat** with subsequent batches of fingers, adding more oil as necessary. Serve hot.

Pumpkin

Yeast Free • Wheat/Gluten Free
Milk/Casein Free • Egg Free • Cholesterol Free
STAGE IV

Cooked pumpkin is delicious as a vegetable side dish, topped with salt and butter or oil, or pureed as the foundation for a pie. It is low in calories and high in flavor!

>   1 pumpkin
>   butter or oil to taste
>   sea salt to taste

To Microwave: Place the whole pumpkin on a microwave safe plate and **cook** on high for 12 minutes. The pumpkin shell should pierce easily and the interior should be soft. if not, cook for another two minutes and test again. Repeat in one minute intervals until the pumpkin is tender. Then, let the pumkin **cool** until you can handle it. **Cut** in half, **scoop** out the seeds and stringy part of the pulp and discard them. Then scoop out the firm pulp from the pumpkin shell. If using the pumpkin for a pie, **puree** in a food processor. If not, **cut** into chunks, melt butter or oil on the pumpkin and sprinkle with salt. **Serve!**

Stovetop Directions: Cut the pumpkin in half. **Scoop out** the seeds and the stringy material holding the seeds together. Set aside. **Place** the pumpkin pieces shell side up in a large pot. **Add** half an inch of water to the pot. **Cover.** Bring to a **boil,** reduce to **simmer** for 30-60 minutes, until the pumpkin is fork-tender. **Cool. Scoop out** the firm pulp. If using for a pie, **puree** in a food processor. If not, **serve hot** with butter or oil and salt.

Directions for Pumpkin, continued. . . . .

Oven directions: Preheat the oven to 350F. **Cut** the pumpkin in halves or quarters. **Scoop out** the seeds and the stringy material holding the seeds together. Set aside. **Place** the pieces of pumpkin on a lightly greased cookie sheet, shell side up. **Bake** at 350F for 30-60 minutes, until the pumpkin is fork-tender. **Cool. Scoop out** the firm pulp. If using for a pie, **puree** in a food processor. If not, **serve hot** with butter or oil and salt.

Pumpkin Seeds

Yeast Free • Wheat/Gluten Free
Milk/Casein Free • Egg Free • Cholesterol Free
STAGE IV

What do you do with all of those pumpkin seeds? Roast and eat them, of course!

Pumpkin seeds from fresh pumpkins
sea salt

Clean the seeds, separating them from the stringy pumpkin pulp. **Spread** on cookie sheets in a single layer. **Sprinkle** with sea salt. **Roast** at 200F until thoroughly dry and crunchy. **Move** the seeds around and **test** about every 30 minutes. If you want **faster results, roast** at 350F, moving the seeds around and testing every 10 minutes. Enjoy!

Notes

Desserts

You can find mouth watering treats in this chapter~~~ easy to make and hard to resist!

Baked Pears & Fruit

Yeast Free • Wheat/Gluten Free
Milk/Casein Free • Egg Free • Cholesterol Free
STAGE IV

This dessert is amazingly simple, but tastes wonderful. It is delicious served alone, or as a sauce over dairy-free ice cream.

> 5 c. fruit
>
> > use blueberries, raspberries, cranberries or blackberries, or a combination of some or all of them
>
> 6 pears, preferably Bartlett
>
> 5 T. natural honey

Preheat the oven to 375F. **Place** the mixed fruit in an ovenproof serving dish. **Mix in** the honey. **Peel and core** the pears, cutting on the stems. Cut them in half. **Lay** the pears over the fruit. **Cover** tightly. **Bake** at 375F for 60-90 minutes, or until the fruit is bubbly pears are cooked through. Serve warm or cold.

Crustless Fruit Pie

Yeast Free • Wheat/Gluten Free
Milk/Casein Free • Egg Free • Cholesterol Free
STAGE IV

When you are craving something sweet and light, try this crustless pie. This makes the equivalent of a 9 inch pie.

> 5 c. fresh or freshly frozen fruit, such as blueberries, cherries, raspberries, cranberries, and/or pears. Mixing is OK
>
> 1/2 c. rice flour
>
> 1/2 c. natural honey
>
> squeeze of fresh lemon juice

Preheat the oven to 350 F. **Mix** the fruit with the rice flour, coating the fruit. **Add** the honey. Mix well. **Add** a squeeze of fresh lemon juice. Put into a pie plate or oven proof dish. **Bake** for about an hour at 350 F, until the fruit bursts open and is bubbling vigorously. This may take longer if you started with frozen fruit. **Cool**. This may be served warm or cold.

Pumpkin, Cranberry and Raspberry Pie

Yeast Free • Wheat/Gluten Free
Milk/Casein Free • Egg Free • Cholesterol Free
STAGE IV

What is Thanksgiving without Pumpkin Pie? This is a very different type of pumpkin pie, using a surprising combination of fruit. Your guests will love it.

2 c. pureed fresh pie pumpkin

1-1/2 c. natural honey

2 c. fresh or freshly frozen cranberries

3 c, fresh or freshly frozen raspberries

1/2 c. rice flour

1 tsp. freshly squeezed lemon juice

10-inch pie crust, plus extra crust for the top (see below)

Preheat the oven to 425 F. **Mix** all ingredients together in a large bowl. If the raspberries are very juicy, pour off the juice and save it for the crust. **Pour** into the rice pie crust. **Press** other pieces of crust dough between your fingers and float them on top of the pie, like a cobbler crust. **Bake** the pie on

top of a cookie sheet (to preserve your oven if the pie overflows) at 425 F. for 15 minutes, then turn down to 350 F for about 40 minutes, or until the fruit is bubbling vigorously.

Mother's Day "Crasberry" Pie

Yeast Free • Wheat/Gluten Free
Milk/Casein Free • Egg Free • Cholesterol Free
STAGE IV

This pie is easy enough to make for mom for Mother's Day, and good enough for even the pickiest moms. This pie can be made with or without the crust.

> Pastry for one double pie crust, 9-inch pie (see recipes in this book and in Feast Without Yeast) (optional)
>
> 2 c. fresh or freshly frozen cranberries, at room temperature
>
> 2 c. fresh or freshly frozen raspberries, at room temperature
>
> 1/3 c. rice flour
>
> 1-1/3 to 1-1/2 c. natural honey
>
> 2 tsp. freshly squeezed lemon juice

Preheat the oven to 375F. **Press** out enough pastry for the bottom crust. Press it into a 9 inch pyrex pie plate. **Prick** the bottom and set aside. Make the filling in a separate bowl: **mix** the berries together. **Add** the flour, mixing well to coat each berry. **Add** the honey. 1-1/3 c. makes a tart pie, 1-1/2 c. makes a sweeter pie. Add the lemon juice. **Mix well.** If making a crustless pie, pour into a bowl suitable for baking and serving, such as a souffle dish. If using a pie crust, pour into the pie crust. **Press** out the pastry for the top crust and lay it over the pie. **Bake** at 375F for 90 minutes, or until the filling is bubbling vigorously.

Spicy Pumpkin Cranberry Pie

Yeast Free • Wheat/Gluten Free
Milk/Casein Free • Egg Free • Cholesterol Free
STAGE IV

This is another exceptional pumpkin pie, with cranberries. This makes enough for a 9 inch pie. This pie is an exception to our general rule against using spices such as cinnamon.

2 c. pureed fresh pie pumpkin
1 c. natural clover honey
1/2 tsp. cinnamon
1/4 tsp. allspice
1/3 c. rice flour
1 c. fresh cranberries
9 inch pie crust or one greased pyrex pie plate

Preheat oven to 425 F. **Mix** with an electric mixer the pumpkin, honey, cinnamon and allspice. **Add** the rice flour; mix well. **Put the cranberries** in a bowl, cover with plastic wrap, and **microwave** on high a minute or two, or until all the berries burst. By hand, **fold** the cranberries into the pumpkin mixture. For a crustless pie, **pour** the filling into a greased pyrex pie plate. For a pie with crust, pour into a 9 inch crust. **Bake** at 425 F for 15 minutes, then decrease heat to 350 F and bake for 45 minutes.

Sweet Rice Pie Crust

Yeast Free • Wheat/Gluten Free
Milk/Casein Free • Egg Free • Cholesterol Free
STAGE IV

This unusual, sweet pie crust is a complement to any fruit pie. Makes enough crust for a 10 inch pie, plus top.

> 1-1/2 c. rice flour
>
> 1 tsp. potato starch baking powder
>
> 1/2 c. frozen butter or expeller pressed safflower oil
>
> 1 T. natural honey
>
> Juice from defrosted raspberries or other fruit (if available), plus enough ice water to make 1 cup of liquid

Put the flour and baking powder in a food processor. **Start processing**. If using butter, **cut** into pieces and drop them in one at a time, continuing to process. If using oil, slowly **pour** it into the flour, continuing to process. **Add** the honey. Slowly **add** the water/juice mixture and process until the dough forms a ball. You might need to stop processing, then **pinch some dough** together with your fingers to see if it sticks together. If so, the dough is done. **Press** the dough into a pyrex pie plate. **Pour** in the filling. Press the remaining crust in pieces between your fingers and float on top of the filling. **Bake** according to directions for the pie.

Butter Rice Pie Crust

Yeast Free • Wheat/Gluten Free
Milk/Casein Free (with butter) • Egg Free
STAGE IV

This pie crust is delicious! Nothing more need be said.

> 1-1/2 c. rice flour
> 1/2 c. butter
> 1 c. ice water

Using a food processor: Put the flour in the mixing bowl of a food processor. Start processing. **Using frozen butter, cut** the butter into pats about 1/8 inch thick. **Drop** in the pats of butter one at a time. The processor will cut the butter into the flour. When all the butter is added, you should have granules of flour. **Gradually add** ice water, starting with a few tablespoons, then adding enough so the flour/butter/ water pastry starts to form a ball. Turn off the processor and test to see if the pastry is ready. When it sticks together and is easy to press out, it is done.

By hand: Put the flour in a bowl. With butter at room temperature, cut the butter into the flour using a pastry blender or two knives. Work the butter and flour until you have pea-sized granules. Gradually mix in the ice water, a few tablespoonsful at a time. When the pastry forms a ball, you are done.

To form a pie crust: press the crust into the bottom on a pie pan (9 inch). For the top crust, press pieces between your fingers and lay the pieces over the pie.

Menus

We have received numerous requests for menus. So here they are! These menus do not by any means use all of the recipes in this book or in *Feast Without Yeast :4 Stages to Better Health*. Nor do these menus exhaust, or even come close to exhausting, the myriad ways in which you can combine recipes to serve meals that will delight your family and company alike. The combinations are endless.

All of the recipes in this chapter are completely yeast free, wheat/gluten free and milk/dairy free. The recipes come from both *Feast Without Yeast* and *Extraordinary Foods for the Everyday Kitchen*. Recipes from *Feast Without Yeast* are marked with a ☆.

You will find most of the recipes are "complete" menus, including soup and salad. They are designed for 6-8 people. If you are serving fewer people, you might eliminate one or more of the dishes.

A note about "Green Salad": we did not include a recipe for a basic green salad, because green salad can be made in so many different ways. Just combine vegetables and lettuce any way you like. In the menus, we say "Green salad" with a certain type of dressing. The page number is for the dressing.

Look through this chapter to find everything you need to get started, from basic suggestions for everyday cooking to more than 60 other menus for:

☆ Everyday Simple Cooking

☆ Vegetarian Main Meals

☆ Main Meals with Meat

☆ Dinners for Company

☆ Special Lunches

☆ The In-Betweeners

☆ Special Occasions

☆ Recipe from *Feast Without Yeast:4 Stages to Better Health.*
All other recipes from *Extraordinary Foods for the Everyday Kitchen.*

Everyday breakfast

Breakfast is the most challenging meal to change from the average American diet. Cereal and milk, toast and eggs--the "normal" foods are out on a yeast-free, wheat-free, dairy-free diet. But breakfast can be great if you expand your horizons! We use potatoes instead of bread, beans instead of eggs. Our regular breakfast is :

Hash Brown Potatoes and Variations   152
Hot beans   ☆ 201
Sliced tomatoes

Everyday lunch

Our everyday lunch is extra food from the night before and from breakfast: containers with whatever bean dish we created the previous night, rice (plain or mixed with safflower oil, salt, and lemon), and a container of hash brown potatoes. Be sure to pack a fork and spoon!

☆Recipe from *Feast Without Yeast:4 Stages to Better Health.*
All other recipes from *Extraordinary Foods for the Everyday Kitchen.*

Everyday Simple Dinners without Meat

The trick to quick cooking for everyday foods is to plan in advance. Put up a slow cooker of beans every night. Then you will have beans for snacks, lunch and dinner when you want them. Put up brown rice each afternoon (or morning) in a rice steamer.   For dinner, when not making one of our other delicious recipes, we drain the slow cooker beans and rinse them. Then we choose a recipe to use, combining the beans with different vegetables and seasonings to create different flavors. We serve the rice plain, or create one of the many fried rice dishes in this book and Feast Without Yeast. Another simple trick is to make baked potatoes in the microwave. Steamed vegetables and a salad round out the meal. For special treats, choose an easy soup to make in a slow cooker. Put it up the night before and relax until dinner time.

Everyday Simple Dinners with Meat

Non-vegetarians can choose any of our meat recipes. Spaghetti and meatballs, Herbed Chicken, and others all are easy to make. Put up rice in a steamer earlier in the day. If you forgot, put some potatoes to bake in the microwave, or yams to bake in the oven with the meat.   Put the meat in the oven. Steam some fresh vegetables. Make a green salad. Voila! You have dinner.

☆Recipe from *Feast Without Yeast:4 Stages to Better Health.*
All other recipes from *Extraordinary Foods for the Everyday Kitchen.*

Vegetarian Main Meals

1

Chili Dilly Soup	✯ 150
Stir-fried Chinese Cabbage	✯ 273
Steamed fresh vegetables	159
South of the Border Pinto Beans	118
Basic Brown Rice	✯ 232
Baked Yams	✯ 258

2

Rainbow Soup	37
Eggplant Pizza-ettes	114
Herbed Brown Rice	✯ 234
or Basic Brown Rice	✯ 232
Steamed Vegetables	159
Wilted Spinach Salad	68

3

Vegetable Split Pea Soup	45
Rice-Ta-Touille	✯ 228
Sweet Rosemary Sauce **over** rice pasta	129
Italian Dressing with green salad	80
Steamed Vegetables	159

✯Recipe from *Feast Without Yeast:4 Stages to Better Health.*
All other recipes from *Extraordinary Foods for the Everyday Kitchen.*

4

Good for What Ails You Onion Soup	*38*
Wilted Spinach Salad	*68*
Fresh Basil and Garlic Sauce	*130*
over rice pasta	
Steamed vegetables	*159*
Gourmet Garbanzos	*123*

5

Fresh Herb, Leek and Butter Sauce	*132*
Sweet and Sour Purple Cabbage	*167*
Basic Lemon Salad Dressing	*74*
with green salad	
Steamed Vegetables	*159*
Stir-fried Broccoli	
and Garbanzo Beans	*120*

6

Another Great Vegetable	
Soup #3	*44*
Sweet Pepper, Tomato, Rosemary	
and Basil Sauce	*134*
over rice pasta	
Steamed vegetables	*159*
Pepper and Cucumber Dressing	*73*
with green salad	
Jeweled Beans	✸ *216*

✸ Recipe from *Feast Without Yeast:4 Stages to Better Health*.
All other recipes from *Extraordinary Foods for the Everyday Kitchen*.

7

South of the Border Pinto Beans	118
Spanish Rice	☆ 229
Roasted Garlic and	
Lemon Dressing	75
with green salad	
Steamed Vegetables	159

   (suggestion: yellow and green summer squash with carrots)

8

Basic Lemon Dressing	74
with green salad	
Cream of Asparagus Soup	☆ 162
Succulent Bell Pepper Sauce	137
over rice pasta	
Sweet and Sour Chinese Vegetables	166
Refried Beans with a Hint of Oregano	117

9

Thick 'N Chunky Tomato Soup	☆ 148
Hummus	☆ 121
Tahini Sauce	85
Falafel	112
Basic Lemon Salad Dressing	74
with green salad	
Stir-Fried Zucchini with Tomatoes	☆ 262
Rice Flatbread	143

☆Recipe from *Feast Without Yeast: 4 Stages to Better Health.*
All other recipes from *Extraordinary Foods for the Everyday Kitchen.*

1

Chili Con Carne	102
Rosemary Roasted Vegetables	160
Steamed Vegetables	
(suggestion:swiss chard)	159
Creamy Cucumber Dressing	☆ 101
with green salad	

2

Cream of Cauliflower Soup	☆ 166
Tarragon Basil Sauce	136
over	
Basic Brown Rice	☆ 232
or rice pasta (spaghetti or fettucine)	
Meatballs & Onions	96
Creamy Cucumber Basil Dressing	77
with green salad	
Steamed green beans	159

3

Cream of Zucchini and Broccoli Soup ☆	160
Roasted Veal	94
Joan's Red Onion Salad Dressing	76
with green salad	
Baked Yams	☆ 258
Steamed asparagus	159

☆Recipe from *Feast Without Yeast:4 Stages to Better Health.*
All other recipes from *Extraordinary Foods for the Everyday Kitchen.*

4

Carrot Ginger Soup	34
Lemon Ginger Chicken	98
Vegetable Fried Rice	☆ 220
Creamy Cucumber Basil Dressing	77
with green salad	

5

Meatballs & Onions	96
Refried Beans with a Hint of Oregano	117
Toasted Rice & Veggies	148
Creamy Cucumber Dressing	☆ 101
with green salad	
Steamed Vegetables	159

6

Rosemary Roasted Vegetables	160
Garlic Beans	☆ 203
Heavenly Salad Dressing	81
with green salad	
Savory Brown Rice	☆ 231
Roasted Chicken with Herbs	☆ 297

☆ Recipe from *Feast Without Yeast:4 Stages to Better Health.*
All other recipes from *Extraordinary Foods for the Everyday Kitchen.*

Dinners for Company

1

Zucchini Lentil Soup	☆ 154
Savory Brown Rice	☆ 231
Creamy Cucumber Dressing	☆ 101
with green salad	
Veal Meatloaf	92
Dad's Favorite Tomato	
and Eggplant Stir-Fry	165
Baked Pears & Fruit	176

2

Carrot Ginger Soup	34
Lemon Salad	64
Chunky Pasta Sauce	127
over rice pasta	
Steamed Vegetables	159

3

Chicken Soup	57
Salad with Fresh Herbs	71
Roasted Eggplant	163
Steamed Artichokes	169
with Celery Seed Mayonnaise	84
Stir-Fried Sugar Snap Peas	164
Sticky Rice	☆ 236
Gourmet Garbanzos	123

☆Recipe from *Feast Without Yeast:4 Stages to Better Health.*
All other recipes from *Extraordinary Foods for the Everyday Kitchen.*

4

Roast Turkey	104
with Thanksgiving Stuffing	✶ 240
Our Favorite Split Pea Soup	✶ 155
Joan's Red Onion Salad Dressing	76
with green salad	
Steamed asparagus	159
Quick 'N Easy Ratatouille	168
Lemony Light Cranberry Sauce	87

5

Rainbow Soup	37
Lemon Salad	64
Falafel	112
Tahini Sauce	85
Basic Brown Rice	✶ 232
Garnish: chopped tomatoes and chopped lettuce	
Rice Flatbread	143

6

Stuffed Cabbage	106
Cream of Zucchini Soup	✶ 158
Heavenly Salad Dressing	81
with green salad	
Rice with Lemon Grass	146
Steamed Vegetables	159

✶Recipe from *Feast Without Yeast:4 Stages to Better Health.*
All other recipes from *Extraordinary Foods for the Everyday Kitchen.*

7

Zesty Eggplant Relish	☆ 276
Baked Rice with Sweet Peppers and Basil	147
Fresh Basil and Oregano Sauce **over** rice pasta	131
Baked Yams	☆ 258
Asparagus Cauliflower Soup	48
Joan's Red Onion Salad Dressing with green salad	76
Steamed vegetables	159

8

Another Great Vegetable Soup #2	43
Sweet & Sour Purple Cabbage	167
Baked Yams	☆ 258
Steamed cauliflower	159
Quick and Easy Pesto **over** rice pasta	128
Basic Lemon Salad Dressing with green salad	74
Mother's Day "Crasberry" Pie	179

9

Cream of Broccoli Soup	☆ 159
Quick 'N Easy Ratatouille	168
Lemon Salad	64
Steamed Vegetables	159
Veal Stew **over** rice or rice pasta	☆ 298
Baked Pears & Fruit	176

☆Recipe from *Feast Without Yeast:4 Stages to Better Health.*
All other recipes from *Extraordinary Foods for the Everyday Kitchen.*

10

Cream of Broccoli Soup	☆ 159
Eggplant Tomato Relish	☆ 277
Heavenly Salad Dressing	81
with green salad	
Sweet and Sour Purple Cabbage	167
Basic Chinese Stir-Fried Vegetables ☆	266
Delectable Tomato Ginger Sauce	133
Sticky Rice	☆ 236

11

Wilted Spinach Salad	68
Cream of Celery Soup	35
Fresh Herb, Leek and Butter Sauce	132
over rice pasta	
Chickenless Chicken with Rice	149
Stir-fried Garbanzo Beans	
with Chinese Long Beans	122

12

Sweet Rosemary Sauce	129
over rice pasta	
South of the Border Pinto Beans	118
Red Rice Soup	46
Sweet Red Pepper Dressing	78
with green salad	
Steamed Vegetables	159
Roasted Eggplant	163

☆Recipe from *Feast Without Yeast:4 Stages to Better Health.*
All other recipes from *Extraordinary Foods for the Everyday Kitchen.*

13

Lemon Ginger Chicken	98
Cream of Cauliflower Soup	★ 166
Mashed Potatoes made with Yukon Gold potatoes	★ 251
Baked Yams	★ 258
Steamed Vegetables	159
Heavenly Salad Dressing with green salad	81

14

Chicken Soup	57
Roasted Chicken with Ginger and Peppers	100
Stir-fried Baby Bok Choy	★ 273
Garbanzo Bean and Pepper Salad	65
Toasted Rice & Veggies	148
Cranberry Pear Sauce	★ 116

15

Pot Roast **with** rice pasta	101
Creamy Cucumber Dressing with green salad	★ 101
Stir Fried Chinese Cabbage	★ 273
Quick 'N Easy Ratatouille	168

★Recipe from *Feast Without Yeast:4 Stages to Better Health.*
All other recipes from *Extraordinary Foods for the Everyday Kitchen.*

1

Up North Potato Salad	69
Quick Sweet Cholent for the Family	55
Lemon Salad	64

2

Asparagus Dill Potato Salad	70
Red Rice Soup	46
Wilted Spinach Salad	68

3

Mediterranean Rice Tabouli	☆ 168
Egg Salad	☆ 170
Pepper and Cucumber Dressing with green salad	73

☆Recipe from *Feast Without Yeast:4 Stages to Better Health*.
All other recipes from *Extraordinary Foods for the Everyday Kitchen*.

4

Parsley Potato Salad	☆ 172
Quick Cholent for the Family	54
Heavenly Salad Dressing	81
with green salad	

5

Cut up fresh vegetables, served with	
Tahini Sauce	85
Hummus	☆ 121
Sweet Super Bowl Salsa	☆ 123
Zucchini and Carrot Soup	49
Fresh Basil and Tomato Salad	72
Rice Flatbread	143

6

Egg Salad	☆ 170
Dilled Potato Salad	☆ 173
Simply Scrumptious Green	
and Red Salad	☆ 179
Basic Tuna Salad	☆ 296

☆Recipe from *Feast Without Yeast: 4 Stages to Better Health.*
All other recipes from *Extraordinary Foods for the Everyday Kitchen.*

1

Lemon Grass Vegetable Soup	40
Mediterranian Rice Tabouli	
(with garbanzo beans)	☆ 168
Stir-Fried Collard Greens	170

2

Cream of Asparagus Soup	☆ 162
Pepper and Cucumber Dressing	73
with green salad	
Rice Flatbread	143

3

Chili Con Carne	102
Creamy Cucumber Basil Dressing	77
with green salad	
Basic Brown Rice	☆ 232

☆Recipe from *Feast Without Yeast:4 Stages to Better Health.*
All other recipes from *Extraordinary Foods for the Everyday Kitchen.*

4

Wilted spinach salad	*68*
Garbanzo Beans with Fresh Peppers	*121*
Fresh Basil and Garlic sauce over rice pasta	*130*

5

Black Bean Salad	*67*
Basic Brown Rice	☆ *232*

6

Asparagus Dill Potato Salad	*70*
Pepper and Cucumber Dressing with green salad	*73*
Carrot, Leek and Broccoli Soup	*36*

☆Recipe from *Feast Without Yeast:4 Stages to Better Health*.
All other recipes from *Extraordinary Foods for the Everyday Kitchen*.

7

Good for What Ails You
    Onion Soup   *38*
Herbed Brown Rice   ☆ *234*
Hot Beans   ☆ *201*
Basic Lemon Dressing   *74*
    with green salad

8

Up North Potato Salad   *69*
Quick Cholent for the Family   *54*
Sweet Red Pepper Dressing   *78*
    with green salad

9

Roasted Garlic and Lemon
    Salad Dressing   *75*
    with green salad
South of the Border Pinto Beans   *118*
Fluffy Rice   ☆ *237*

☆Recipe from *Feast Without Yeast:4 Stages to Better Health.*
All other recipes from *Extraordinary Foods for the Everyday Kitchen.*

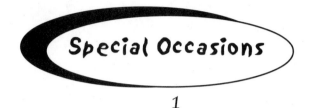

Special Occasions

1

Channukah Party Buffet Menu

This is a menu for a large buffet, 30-40 people.
For fewer people, make fewer dishes.

Mixed vegetables, cut up
   Dip:
   Celery Seed Mayonnaise   *84*
choice of
   Creamy Cucumber Dressing   ⭐ *101*
   Joan's Red Onion Dressing   *76*
   with green salad
Crispy Potato Latkes
   Without Eggs or Wheat   ⭐ *256*
Soft 'N Spicy Potato Latkes,
   without Wheat or Eggs!   ⭐ *254*
Pear Sauce   ⭐ *120*
Lemony Light Cranberry Sauce   *87*
Steamed fresh green beans   *159*
Egg Salad   ⭐ *170*
Fresh Basil and Tomato Salad   *72*
Mediterranean Rice Tabouli   ⭐ *168*
   Dessert:

Crustless Fruit Pie   *177*
Fresh fruit, in season

⭐Recipe from *Feast Without Yeast:4 Stages to Better Health.*
All other recipes from *Extraordinary Foods for the Everyday Kitchen.*

2

Birthday Dinner #1

Carrot Ginger Soup	34
Lemon Salad	64
Chickenless Chicken and Rice	149
Stir-Fried Sugar Snap Peas	164
Dad's Favorite Tomato and Eggplant Stir Fry	165
Pumpkin, Cranberry and Raspberry Pie	178
Birthday Sorbet Cake	☆ 358

3

Birthday Dinner #2

Basic Lemon Salad Dressing with green salad	74
Lemon Roasted Potatoes	☆ 244
Steamed Vegetables	159
Quick and Easy Pesto served over rice pasta	128
Gourmet Garbanzos	123
Baked Pears & Fruit	176

☆Recipe from *Feast Without Yeast:4 Stages to Better Health.*
All other recipes from *Extraordinary Foods for the Everyday Kitchen.*

4

Menu for a Holiday Meal #1

for 12-15 guests

Rainbow Soup	37
Heavenly Salad Dressing	81
with green salad	
Gefilte Fish	☆ 292
Stuffed Cabbage	106
Rice pasta	
Veggie Potato Bake	150
Rosemary Roasted Vegetables	160
Baked Pears and Fruit	176
Blueberry Sorbet	☆ 352

5

Menu for a Holiday Meal #2

for 12-15 guests

Chicken Soup	57
with Vegetarian Matzo Balls	☆ 144
Gefilte Fish	☆ 292
Creamy Cucumber Dressing	☆ 101
with green salad	
Chicken & Vegetables	99
Vegetarian Baked Beans	☆ 210
Baked Potatoes	156
Rice Flatbread	143

☆Recipe from *Feast Without Yeast:4 Stages to Better Health.*
All other recipes from *Extraordinary Foods for the Everyday Kitchen.*

6

Mostly Vegetarian Passover Feast
for 15-20 guests

Haroset for Passover	☆ 119
Gefilte Fish	☆ 292
Eggplant Tomato Relish	☆ 277
Vegetable garnish	
Vegetable Soup for Matzah Balls	☆ 142
with Vegetarian Matzah Balls	☆ 144
Roasted Garlic	
and Lemon Salad Dressing	75
with green salad	
Cranberry Tzimmes	154
*Chickenless Chicken and Rice	149
*Garbanzo Beans with Fresh Peppers	121
Lemon Roasted Potatoes	☆ 244
Steamed Vegetables	159
Baked Pears & Fruit	176

*These recipes contain "kitniot." Check with your rabbi to determine whether you should include them in your Passover meal.

7

Special Chicken Dinner

Chicken & Vegetables	99
Baked Acorn Squash with Honey	157
Toasted Rice & Veggies	148
Steamed Vegetables	159
Red Rice Soup	46
Creamy Cucumber Dressing	☆ 101
with green salad	

☆Recipe from *Feast Without Yeast:4 Stages to Better Health.*
All other recipes from *Extraordinary Foods for the Everyday Kitchen.*

8

Thanksgiving Feast

for 12-15 guests

Roast Turkey, stuffed with	*104*
Thanksgiving Stuffing	☆ *240*
Veal Stuffing Casserole	*91*
Lemony Light Cranberry Sauce	*87*
or Cranberry Fruit Sauce	☆ *118*
Baked Yams	☆ *258*
or Stir-Fried Yams and Ginger	*155*
Lemon Roasted Potatoes	☆ *244*
Sweet Red Pepper Dressing	*78*
with green salad	
Steamed Vegetables	*159*

Dessert--Choice of:

Spicy Non-Dairy Pumpkin Pie Filling	☆ *332*
Thanksgiving Pie	☆ *334*
Spicy Pumpkin Cranberry Pie	*180*
Pumpkin, Cranberry and	
Raspberry Pie	*178*
Baked Pears & Fruit	*176*

☆Recipe from *Feast Without Yeast:4 Stages to Better Health.*
All other recipes from *Extraordinary Foods for the Everyday Kitchen.*

9

The 4 Stages meet the "Low Carb" Diet

This is a low-carb, high meat protein menu that makes a special meal for people following those types of regimens. We offer this as a way to expand your repertoire for your guests. We do not endorse or recommend such diets.

Roast Turkey	104
stuffed with Vegetable Stuffing	161
Good for What Ails You Onion Soup	38
Creamy Cucumber Dressing	☆ 101
with green salad	
Steamed Vegetables	159
Mother's Day Crasberry	
Pie, made without crust	179

10

Sumptuous Chinese Vegetarian Dinner

Chinese Tomato Soup	41
Sweet & Sour Chinese Vegetables	166
Stir-Fried Yams and Ginger	155
Stir-fried Sugar Snap Peas	164
Sticky Rice	☆ 236

☆Recipe from *Feast Without Yeast: 4 Stages to Better Health.*
All other recipes from *Extraordinary Foods for the Everyday Kitchen.*

11

Mediterranean Brunch

Hummus	✱ 121
Chopped tomatoes and cucumbers, with Basic Lemon Salad Dressing	74
Mediterranean Rice Tabouli	✱ 168
Sweet and Sour Purple Cabbage	167
Egg Salad	✱ 170
Asparagus Dill Potato Salad	70
Cut up vegetables with choice of dips:	
Basil Mayonnaise	84
Pepper and Cucumber Dressing	73
Fresh berries in season	

12

Vegetarian New Year's Dinner

Carrot Ginger Soup	34
Lemon Salad	64
Pizza	110
Stir-Fried Collard Greens	170
Sweet and Soup Purple Cabbage	167
Gourmet Garbanzos	123

✱Recipe from *Feast Without Yeast:4 Stages to Better Health.*
All other recipes from *Extraordinary Foods for the Everyday Kitchen.*

13

Taco Feast #1!

Rainbow Soup	*37*
Tacos	*108*
Taco Sauce	
Taco Bean Filling and/or Taco Veal Filling	
Guacamole	*82*
Rice Flatbread	*143*
Garnish: chopped lettuce, chopped tomatoes	
Basic Lemon Salad Dressing with green salad	*74*
Steamed Vegetables	*159*
Toasted Rice & Veggies	*148*

14

Taco Feast #2!

Wilted Spinach Salad	*68*
Chinese Tomato Soup	*41*
Guacamole	*82*
Tacos	*108*
Taco Sauce	
Taco Bean Filling and/or Taco Veal Filling	
Baked Yams	✫ *258*
Rice Flatbread	*143*
Tomato Rice	✫ *230*
Garnish: shredded lettuce, shredded tomatoes	
Baked Pears & Fruit	*176*

✫Recipe from *Feast Without Yeast:4 Stages to Better Health.*
All other recipes from *Extraordinary Foods for the Everyday Kitchen.*

15

Summer Taco Feast

Cool Cream of Cucumber Soup	☆ 165
Lemon Salad	64
Hot Salsa!	86
Rice Flatbread	143
Tacos:	108

Mild Taco Sauce
Taco Bean filling
Taco Meat Filling
Garnish: shredded lettuce, chopped
tomatoes

Chickenless Chicken and Rice	149
Steamed vegetables	159

☆Recipe from *Feast Without Yeast:4 Stages to Better Health.*
All other recipes from *Extraordinary Foods for the Everyday Kitchen.*

Quick Order Form

Mail Orders: Wisconsin Institute of Nutrition, LLP, 5555 No. Port Washington Road,Suite 200, Glendale, WI 53217

Telephone Credit Card Orders: Toll-Free 1-877-332-7899; local or long distance: (414) 351-1194

An Extraordinary Power to Heal	$24.95	_____	$_____
Extraordinary Foods for the *Everyday Kitchen*	$15.95	_____	$_____
Feast Without Yeast	$22.95	_____	$_____
Sales Tax: 5.6% Wisconsin Residents			$_____
Shipping: $5.50 for First Book + $3.50 for each add'l to same address			$_____
		Total:	$_____

Please call 1-877-332-7899 for shipping rates for orders outside US.
Please call for special discounts for large orders.

Payment: _____Check _____Visa _____Mastercard

Credit Card Number: _____

Expiration Date: _____/_____

Zip Code of Billing Address for Credit Card: _____

Ship To:

Name: _____

Address: _____

City: _____State: _____ Zip: _____

Phone Number: _____ email: _____